CAMPAIGN
to be a
BETTER LEADER

12 Essential Keys for Unlocking Leadership Excellence

GARY BERGENSKE

CAMPAIGN to be a BETTER LEADER
12 Essential Keys for Unlocking Leadership Excellence
by Gary Bergenske
Copyright Gary Bergenske
All Rights Reserved.
ISBN: 978-1-59755-172-4

Published By: ADVANTAGE BOOKS
advbookstore.com

This book and parts thereof may not be reproduced in any form, stored in a retrieval system, or transmitted in any form by any means (electronic, mechanical, photocopy, recording, or otherwise) without prior written permission from the author, except as provided by the United States of America copyright law.

Library of Congress Control Number: 2008941790

Edited by, Leslie Kressel Johnson, Orlando, Florida

Photographs by; Jon Thomas Gumina of Jon Thomas Photography, Sanford, Florida

Graphic design by; Jason Bergenske, Maitland, Florida

Cover by: Pat Theriault

First Printing: December 2008
25 26 27 28 29 30 31   10 9 8 7 6 5 4 3

Endorsements

Praise For
Campaign To Be A Better Leader

"In a world packed with leadership books, **Gary Bergenske** has written a classic. You will be a far more effective leader after you read and digest this book."

Pat Williams
Orlando Magic Senior Vice President
Author of *"The Pursuit"*

"Fresh, insightful, and heartwarming... with ***Campaign To Be A Better Leader,*** Gary touches upon topic matter that virtually anyone will find useful in their own personal quests for excellence both in business and in life."

Katherine Phelps.
CEO/PUBLISHER
BEAUTIFUL MEDIA, LLC

"In the recent past, I have taken some leadership classes and read some good leadership books. I believe this book of Gary's is one of the best as it is so easy to read and understand. A must read!"

Happy Schuur
Crittenden Fruit Co., Inc.
Treasurer

"***Campaign to be a Better Leader*** is synonymous with leadership. ***Gary Bergenske's*** book will give you skills to become better in every setting you practice leadership. Highly recommended."

Bob Poston
Sekco Energy, Inc
President & CEO

"Gary's title says it all this time. Leadership is a dynamic thing, requiring constant evaluation and daily nurturing. Leadership is a daily campaign. Read to Lead!"

Tom Storm, Account Executive
National Van Lines, Inc.

"Leadership is one of those vague concepts which has thousands of definitions, examples, and ways of being exhibited. What works for one individual may completely flop for another. Yet, there are essential concepts that are the solid foundation of all leadership and success-and no one knows this better than Gary Bergenske. ***Campaign To Be A Better Leader*** not only teaches those elements of powerful leadership, but gives examples and experiences which tie everything together in an easy-to-understand form. Better yet, these concepts are ready to be implemented into your daily life-right here, right now, no excuses!"

Marcus Engel
Professional Speaker and Author
Author of "After This"

"I have spent much of my career in retail management. As I began to read **Campaign to be a Better Leader,** I saw the different ways I have personally changed in my leadership roles. This book will have a huge impact on your life, career, and relationships with others. The twelve keys are a powerful list of guidelines to help guide you to answer the call to true leadership. Gary's book should be a must read for any individual who is serious about becoming an effective leader."

Robert Amico
Shriners Hospitals for Children, Tampa
Board of Governors

"You can feel the energy and excitement of **Gary's** words. His writing truly inspires you to want to work toward the goal of reaching excellence. Gary is a perfect example of someone who has a positive outlook on everything he is involved in. He has a strong positive influence with everyone he meets."

 Michael G. Juett,
VP/Owner Skycraft Parts & Surplus, Inc.

"I am so excited about the publication of your second book. The first one was the only complete book I have read in 25 years, now this one is even better. Everyone should take the time to read it if interested in leadership."

George Barfield, Owner
Conway Village Barber Shop

Gary Bergenske

Gary and Anne Bergenske in one of the promotional photos used in Gary's campaign for an office with Shriners International and Shriners Hospitals for Children.

Gary Bergenske

Dedication

To my mother, Rose, who guided me with love.

To my wife, Anne, who has shown me the meaning of love.

To our six children, who have given me the joy of love.

To the memory of my father, Jim, who impressed upon me, "When your character is one of integrity," you will be loved.

Gary Bergenske

Table of Contents

Dedication 9

Foreword 13

Introduction 15

Acknowledgements 19

Preface 21

Chapter One 23
BELIEVE In Everything You Do

Chapter Two 35
Surround Yourself With Excellence

Chapter Three 47
VISION with the Ability to Make it Happen

Chapter Four 57
Organizing the Mission and Chasing the Goal

Chapter Five 67
Leaders Know How to COACH

Chapter Six 77
COMMUNICATING for Positive Results

Chapter Seven 87
PASSION Leads You to the Top

Chapter Eight 97
PERSISTENCE: Make It Your Way of Life

Chapter Nine 107
Earning Loyalty and Respect

Chapter Ten 117
Embracing Change Builds Leaders

Chapter Eleven 127
Team Effort Accelerates Success

Chapter Twelve 137
Keeping the Momentum Looking to the Future

Conclusion 147
Ten Steps to Becoming a Better Leader

About the Author 151

Foreword

When this book, *"Campaign to be a Better Leader,"* was written I didn't know much about the author, **Gary Bergenske**. We had a mutual friend who asked me to write the foreward for this book. My first reaction was, "No. I am too busy, I don't know the author well enough, and it would be unfair to his readers and his book for me to even consider it."

Our mutual friend was quite persistent and began to enumerate about the great qualities of Gary as a businessman, a father, a husband, a member of the Board of Directors for Shriners Hospitals, and overall as a good person. It was obvious our mutual friend would not take no for an answer. I thought if he believed in Gary that much the least I could do was read it and then make a decision. In other words, this would give me a legitimate reason to say no. But, I could rationalize to myself that I based my decision on the content of the book and not on my schedule.

I received a rough draft of the book and read it. As I worked my way through the book, my attitude changed as I became aware that the contents of the book could be of great value to its readers. In the book, Gary enumerates on the lessons of leadership he learned and experienced as a leader of his successful company, J & J Metro Moving and Storage Co., a motivational speaker, one of the leaders of the Shriners, a husband, and a father of six children 20-30 years of age.

Because you are a president of a company, or a father, does not make you a leader. The other day, my wife asked, "Are you born a leader or is that a trait that can be learned?" Without hesitation I said, "Anyone can learn to become a leader." This book will show you how to become a leader.

Gary will expand upon the twelve steps you need to work on to become a better leader. I like to think I am a leader. However, as I was reading this book, I often found myself saying, "I wish I had known this 30 years ago." There is no doubt in my mind that Gary's book caused me to think how I could have been a better leader.

His book covers such salient points as you must make a commitment to being a leader, believe in yourself and your team, strive for excellence, get the most out of your team, communicate, be persistent, embrace changes, act to get people to work together, and many other valuable traits a leader must possess.

I personally found the book to be well-written, easy to read and understand, and filled with a ton of information.

One last thought before you read this book - get a pencil and notepad as I am certain you will take many notes. Enjoy the book and congratulations on taking an important step to being a better leader. Oh, by the way, you may want to pack a snack as you will have trouble putting the book down.

    Lou Holtz
    ESPN Studio Analyst
    Former New York Jets Head Coach
    Former College Football Head Coach

Introduction

As I look back on my life, great leaders have always influenced me and many of my decisions. Looking back at the many critical challenges I have faced, the outcomes were the result of the preparation process learned from past and current leaders in my life. On the flipside, even the joyful decisions were influenced by others, as great leaders live in their leadership role all of the time, and live their life accordingly.

Leadership should start with your parents, and then move to teachers and coaches. As a 16-year-old young man working in a restaurant, my first employer was a tremendous leader who instilled in me the tenants of hard work. His leadership provided me with the self-confidence to achieve more. Those of us who have had the opportunity to work among other great leaders are sure to benefit if we so desire. Each leader anyone has worked under has provided some influence on their life. Our rate of success depends on what we retain from those from whom we have learned.

Leaders are needed in every aspect of life. I admire leaders who have the support of their followers, and who have the ability to make other's lives better. It is not an easy task to be a person who can persuade people to do more. However, good leaders thrive on encouraging others to do more than they ever imagined possible. Leaders become permanent students of their profession, building teams of successful people.

For years, sales was my business, but I had always dreamed of owning my own business. I focused on my goal, worked on my leadership skills, and went to work. Twelve years later, in 1985, I purchased **J & J Metro**, a moving and storage company in Orlando, Florida. I didn't know much about the moving and storage business, but knew it involved leading and dealing with people and sales. A company needs good employees to grow; therefore, you must communicate, as the leader or boss, to your employees the benefits to all of hard work and good service.

The people of J & J Metro have worked hard with me to insure its growth. As time goes on, you look for other avenues to find success in leadership, as success in business is only one part of life. There is also success found in family, church, and the community.

With a wonderful wife, Anne, and six children, I am fortunate to have a successful family life. As for community, I have my church, civic groups, and a volunteer fraternal organization, The Shriners. The Shriners is best known as the group of men who wear funny red hats and drive small cars in parades, but this is only a small part of what their fraternity and philanthropy provide. The Shriners are devoted to service to the community.

Across the United States, Canada, and Mexico, there are 22 Shriners Hospitals for Children. These hospitals treat children with catastrophic burn injuries, orthopedic problems, and spinal cord injuries. There is no charge to any of these children's families because these men in the funny red hats raise hundreds of millions of dollars to pay for construction of the facilities and treatment for the children.

My greatest accomplishment in life was being elected by the members of the Shrine fraternity to an International office. As a member of the Boards of Directors for the **Shriners of North America and Shriners Hospitals for Children**, a 21-member body that helps govern the Shriners fraternity and hospitals, I have found great compassion in giving back. As a member of these boards, there is no pay. All time is donated. It's not about money; it's about leadership and giving children better lives.

Reading this book will bring you to realize how leadership is not about power, position, or an inflated ego. Rather, you will come to understand that the greatest of leaders are those who lead by influence - through methods of motivating others with passion to be better even than they themselves thought they could be. The true value of a leader is not judged while serving, but it is determined by how those he has influenced perform once he is no longer there.

In this book you will find key ideas and proven principals that will unlock your mind, so your leadership skills will flourish. Each chapter will inspire you to dream, and to turn those dreams into leadership action that will take you to success. You will come to understand the importance of being a leader, the respect you will gain, and the opportunities you will have to give back. These key principals will help you to make significant changes in your life that will, in turn, improve the lives of others.

The book covers 12 important aspects for improving your leadership skills. Each chapter contains suggestions and examples to help guide you to fulfillment. Each chapter stands on its own, allowing you to use it as a handy daily reference guide or to share with friends. I'm asking you to make the commitment to become a better leader for the benefit of those around you.

Whether you wish to improve your leadership skills personally or as part of a team, you will enjoy this book. A new focus will emerge in your thinking of leading people. Your life will be improved. Sit down and begin reading. Take notes and share your new found knowledge with others. Be all you can be in life. Others are depending on you. When it comes to dreaming of **becoming a better leader,** this is an excellent place to start. Just start reading and enjoy!

Gary Bergenske

Acknowledgements

I am grateful to Anne, my wife, for her support and understanding as I have chased my dreams to become a better leader. Through her confidence, she has assisted me in growing as a person. Without her belief in my dreams, this journey would not have been possible.

I'm extremely thankful to Leslie Kressel Johnson who spent many hours editing this book. Her professional talents have improved the quality of this book. I have enjoyed our relationship and my experience working with her.

I acknowledge with deep appreciation all of my Shriner colleagues whose friendships and input have aided in the writing of this book. Their encouragement and camaraderie have inspired me in creating this book, allowing me to improve my life. Now, I share what I've learned with everyone.

Gary Bergenske

Preface

The need for great leaders has become more important than ever. With the world constantly changing and competition growing stronger by the day, leaders are in demand. The future depends on the leadership qualities of those individuals who focus on getting others to do their best and make things happen. Good leadership has become a must for individuals, teams, and groups not only to move ahead; it is required to merely stay status quo with where they are.

It has become compulsory for anyone striving to rise to a leadership position to partake in leadership development on a regular basis. Expecting that others will follow you without your making a concerted effort at self-improvement simply will not happen. You must become a willing student of leadership if you are to advance. An open mind with the ability to accept change will allow you to advance as a leader. Along the way, you will find their position in the world actually has little to do with the greatest of leaders. Throughout history, the leaders who made the biggest impact were those who led with passion - passion so strong the influence they had on their followers became captivating.

I have witnessed many leaders in my business, in other's businesses, and in the 191 Shriners' Chapters throughout North America for which I serve on the Board of Directors. Leaders, some of them highly skilled and some still developing their skills, come in many variations. Within the Shriners organization, all of the members, as well as the leaders, are volunteers. This in itself challenges and transforms leaders of any skill level to be at their best if they wish others to follow them. In a volunteer setting, only those leaders who keep others happy, while keeping them motivated, will be successful in keeping them returning for more. I firmly believe people leading in a volunteer setting, where they are not paid, is the truest test of a good leader's abilities. It is my mission to help those individuals who wish to become better leaders by sharing the information accumulated in this book.

My position with the Shriners of North America has taken me on many trips. In these travels, I have found some leaders who lead with ease, while others have to work at it daily. Either way, much of what makes the great ones great is their ability to inspire, to motivate, and to coach with passion those who want to improve themselves to become leaders. Having leaders willing to lead others to be as good as or better than themselves is what makes organizations great, especially when leaders serve a finite term - when they must turn over the reins to the next person in line. Unselfish leaders, whose focus is on the betterment of the team and not only themselves, are the ones who progress the farthest.

It has been my pleasure to write this book. It is my sincere wish that it will help many people raise themselves to a level where they will become better leaders. My dream is they will pass this information on to others they influence, who themselves will become better leaders, and so on and so on. The guidelines, examples, and techniques for improving leadership skills are accumulated here in easy reading form to allow you to ***Campaign to be a Better Leader.*** It all begins with your commitment to reading this book. Soon after, you will be feeling the rewards and benefits of performing as a ***Better Leader!***

    Gary Bergenske
    Maitland, Florida

Chapter One

BELIEVE
In Everything You Do

*"You must first be a believer,
If you are to be an achiever"*
Unknown

Believe! It is a required ingredient in every successful task you undertake. My first experience with the power of believing took place at the young age of eleven. It was 1965; I had a dream of competing and winning in the Ford PP&K-the Ford Punt, Pass and Kick football competition. Young boys would compete separately in four age divisions (8-9, 10-11, 12-13, 14-15), with the top three performers in each group being awarded a prized plaque. All participants would launch one punt, one pass, and one kick, with scores based on distance and accuracy (in feet). I yearned to win one of those plaques, but felt it was out of reach for my ability.

That is when my father had his first talk with me about believing in myself. He told me, *"Anything was possible by setting a goal, properly preparing for it, and then giving it everything you had."* He also said, *"If you're going to be an achiever, you must first believe you can do it."*

I practiced daily with that old football in our long gravel driveway—kicking it one way, chasing it down, passing it back, and punting it again. Often working with no one but myself, I spent more time chasing the ball than I did practicing. As my preparations continued for the big day of competition, my belief that a win was possible continued to increase. I was kicking a long one more consistently and feeling stronger as I found additional strength from my belief. Soon, I realized there were no limitations as to what could happen—if I continued to believe, nothing was impossible.

The competition was held on a fall Saturday afternoon in the small town of Pardeeville, Wisconsin. Although it was over 40 years ago, I remember it as if it were yesterday. The cool day found many young boys like me there with their fathers, each of them with the desire to do their best. My small hand was not capable of firmly palming the ball for the pass, but I threw it right down the middle for good yardage. My punt was high and off to the left, costing me some yardage. It was down to the place kick. It had to have good distance if I were to be in the running. I believed I could accomplish it. Due to my preparation, my confidence was high. I teed up the ball, stepped back, and focused. One, two, three, *kick!* The contact was perfect; it was the best kick I had ever made.

At the end of the day when all the scores were in, my first exercise in believing in myself resulted in the second place plaque. The following day in the local newspaper, a story on the event in part said, "The longest kick of the day came from Gary Bergenske, a smaller boy in one of the younger age groups."

You can imagine my excitement as an eleven-year-old. My first lesson in believing in myself rewarded me with a lifetime memory I have thought of often. Thomas Jefferson said, "I'm a great **believer** in luck, and I find the harder I work, the more I have of it." Looking back, it was my father's belief in me and his guidance to assist me to get in shape for the competition that won it. Nothing more, nothing less. It was all about his belief in me and being prepared. That's what gave me the confidence to believe in myself.

> *"I'm a great believer in luck,*
> *And I find the harder I work,*
> *The more I have of it."*
> **Thomas Jefferson**

By definition, the word **"believe"** means *to accept as true or truthful*, or, *to be of the opinion that something exists or is a reality, especially when there is no absolute proof of its existence or reality*. The word **"believe"** is an inspirational word often used in a religious setting and has been the key word in many songs. Neil Diamond composed the song **"I'm A Believer,"** recorded by the band The Monkees in 1966. One year later, The Monkees recorded another song, **"Daydream Believer."** Both songs hit number one on the U. S. Billboard Hot 100 chart. Cher's **"Believe,"** the biggest hit of her career, was the number one song for 15 weeks in 1998, giving it one of the longest runs ever at number one.

The word "believe" has a fascination or mystery about it. What do you believe is true, even though you cannot prove it?

In Anaheim, California, Disneyland is a place where dreams and imagination are around every corner. In the year 2000 as part of its 45th anniversary celebration, this inspirational place began using a new theme, **Believe...There's Magic in the Stars,** for its popular evening fireworks show. This fireworks show was so popular it ran until late 2004.

I share these bits of information and short stories with you to show the importance *believing* has in every person's life. How each of us longs for the qualities believing brings to our lives. The faith, the dreams, the trust, and the imagination a believer has will take him to new destinations in life. When it comes to this subject, I only hope that each of you believe in yourself as much as I believe in you.

If you dream of taking on new challenges, you have to believe in yourself. The problem is that many people do not. They doubt their thoughts and second guess their ambitions. It is imperative you become a person of positive thinking if you plan to become a *believer*. Following is a list of ten recommended thought processes for every believer to focus on in building their character:

10 Character Traits of Believers

1. **Is Dedicated** – Is wholeheartedly devoted to a goal, cause, or dream.
2. **Has Faith in Others** – Belief in, devotion to, or trust in somebody or something, especially without logical proof. Has strongly held set of principles.
3. **Stays Committed** – Remains entrusted and steadfast. Is unwavering and persistent in reaching the goal.

4. **Strives to Succeed** – Tries hard to make significant progress to accomplish successful results. Looks for a specific, measurable, positive outcome.
5. **Builds Confidence** – Develops faith in own talents. Has a self-assurance that his views and abilities are of value to others.
6. **Intellectually Akin** - Having a highly developed ability to think, reason, and understand related subjects, especially in combination with a wide knowledge, rather than using emotions.
7. **Is Trustful and Loyal** – Can be relied upon by others to behave responsibly and honorably, remaining faithful to a country, person, ruler, government, or ideal. Is dependable and dedicated to a cause.
8. **Can Accept Things to be True** – Can acknowledge that something is real or genuine prior to being able to prove it. Has the ability to see the big picture before being able to justify or authenticate it.
9. **Has Faith in Himself or Herself** – Is able to trust his/her own actions based on loyalty to self and prior successes. Has the ability to stay committed, resulting in a sense of responsibility or devotion to duty that builds self esteem.
10. **Can Visualize the Future** – Is willing to create a vivid, positive, mental picture of an event that has not yet happened, such as a desired outcome to a problem or challenge, in order to promote a sense of well-being. Dreams of opportunities with measurable goals.

True believers have unique qualities, allowing them to look into the future with their imagination to see what could be. True believers also have the stamina and the wherewithal to churn out the necessary effort to make what they believe in a reality. You cannot persuade a believer, for his belief is not based on evidence; it is based on a firmly unseated need to believe. Believers will go the extra mile, work the extra hours, and make the needed sacrifices to ensure that what they believe in is successful.

Do you believe in miracles? I've seen too many not to. Miracles usually come to fruition because someone believed they would. It has also been said that there are no miracles for those who do not believe in them. This again accentuates the power of believing. So, believe in yourself and all you do. Believers are miracle-makers, and they know nothing is impossible. There is no difficulty that cannot be overcome. Believers know that our only limitations are those we put on ourselves.

Never believe in defeat. If you have your eye on the goal, you'll find a way . . . if you don't, you'll find an excuse.

Believe In Others, It's Contagious

The quality of believing in others is a trait that will build your character in the eyes of others. If you have the vision to believe in another person before he is successful, you will be of great benefit to that person. Believing and inspiring someone who has not yet made the grade requires the ability to see the undeveloped potential in another person. In sharing your belief in others, you take on a role of motivating them to have further belief in themselves, thereby promoting additional momentum. Believing breeds *hope* and *faith* that results in a desired outcome.

Everyone is eager to jump on the bandwagon and believe in a winner. I have seen it many times with sports teams and in groups. If a team is losing, the supporters are thin and the naysayers are out. However, if they put together a little winning streak, believers suddenly appear. A true believer sticks with it through thick and thin. Temporary set backs are not of concern, and only the focus on the big picture is what matters.

I have found a few excellent tools that work in supporting others to believe in themselves. By believing passionately in something that does not exist, it can be created. When using these methods of inspiring others to believe in themselves, they will also believe in their dreams. Each of these tools will keep them on track, *believing it is true and possible,* even though it cannot be proven.

- **Keep the Faith**
- **Expect Success**
- **See Beyond Proof**
- **Be Understanding**
- **Visualize Together**
- **Give Self-Assurance**
- **Record Past Successes**
- **Positive Reinforcement**
- **Listen to Their Dreams**
- **Encourage after a Failure**

In leadership, believing in others is a powerful tool. It will consistently inspire others to achieve more than they thought possible as they make every effort to live up to your expectations. Often, simply because the leader believes it is possible, the unthinkable becomes believable to all others on the team. Good leaders are capable of breaking down the difficult into smaller, achievable, believable tasks. In doing so, you will soon find the entire team accepting the challenge with confidence, all because their leader believed in them. Believing in each other is what makes a team greater than the sum of its individuals. **If you want**

results you have never had, you must believe in what you have never done.

I have been an Orlando Magic season ticket holder since they tipped off the first ball. A few years ago, they had this campaign slogan for the year—**BELIEVE**. Every advertisement, every media ad, and all the hype at the arena was focused around this one word. Believe.

It was an ad campaign that brought with it *excitement, hope, desire,* and *focus*. This one word woke up Orlando as they **"Believed in Magic."** Their team made a run not just at the playoffs, but for a championship. Each player and fan gazed confidently towards a reality that could be, if they would just *believe*. They did not win the championship that year, but believe me, they gave it one heck of an exciting run. The Magic found a bit of magic in believing and convinced every fan that if they would believe, anything was possible. It was an excellent display of what a team could do by believing.

Believe in Yourself, It Is Essential to Prosper

When it comes to believing in yourself, Norman Vincent Peale—clergyman, motivational speaker and writer—had this to say, **"Believe in yourself! Have faith in your abilities! Without a humble but reasonable confidence in your own powers you cannot be successful or happy."**

It seems odd that so many people can believe in others, and yet when it comes to believing in themselves, they fail. Many are so hard on their own beliefs they become self-discouraged. This leads to putting a small price on your ideas. If you get caught in this trap, rest assured that others will not put any higher value on you, either. You, personally, have to believe in your dreams and aspirations if you wish others to believe in you and your future.

Nobody Can Make You Feel Inferior Without Your Consent

Experiencing little successes along the way builds confidence, faith, and trust in your self-worth. By first applying good judgment, then having the good sense to research and test your ideas and dreams, you will develop an attitude of why it should work as opposed to why it should not. In doing so, you will find it easier and easier to become a believer. As you begin to believe in your ideas, you will also begin to grow in how you feel about yourself.

Eleanor Roosevelt said, ***"Nobody can make you feel inferior without your consent."*** Believe in everything you do. Even if it does not turn out the way you planned, you will come one step closer to finding the solution, as you have eliminated another way it will not work. Part of being a believer is knowing how to rebound from defeat or failure with renewed excitement for success. Many great ideas have fallen undeveloped, when they were attainable had only continued belief prevailed.

Believing in one's self requires self-control, poise, and vision. This is essential to becoming a persuasive, influential leader and to having others believe in you and your ideas. All great leaders believe with intensity until they become passionate about their dreams, goals, and ideas. Leaders have an attitude of making a difference, and are not satisfied until they do. Believe in yourself, and your dreams will come true. Be a leader . . . *believe*.

Believe in the Team, Success Requires Every Member

For team participation to peak and be successful takes each and every member operating at 100 percent. In order for this to happen, each member has to believe in his teammates. In the business world, corporations have high expectations on the results from other departments. In the sports world, team members trust others to do their part. The quarterback believes in his blockers and receivers. The pitcher believes in his catcher. If, at any time, they do not believe in each other, there is a break down in quality. It may be minor; however, it causes performance to be less than 100 percent. The members of great teams believe in their coaches, their teammates, and their mission. They make it happen.

Of all the team activities I have ever witnessed, the one that exemplifies belief in each other most is one that, if not performed perfectly, could cause death. I am talking about a family that has performed together for seven generations, losing some family members to death along the way. Even with the greatest sacrifice of all, human life, they have continued to believe in themselves, in each other, and in their mission. I first saw this astonishing family, "The Flying Wellendas," at a Shrine Circus several years ago. Balancing on a tight wire many feet above the ground, each member places his or her life in the belief of other's ability to perform with perfection. This is extraordinary belief in others at its best, and is witnessed by hundreds of thousands as their circus act travels the country.

According to their Web site, the 1920's act toured Europe for several years and featured an amazing 4-person, 3-level pyramid. Two men would ride bicycles on a wire 50 feet in the air, while Karl Wellenda precariously balanced on a chair on top of a bar on their shoulders. At the same time, Helen would stand on Karl's shoulders! This act was such a sensation that when John Ringling saw them performing in Cuba, he immediately contracted them to appear with the **"Greatest Show On Earth."** When the Great Wallendas debuted their act (without a net—it had been misplaced in shipping) at Madison Square Garden in 1928, they received a standing ovation that lasted 15 minutes!

Never before nor to date has applause stopped a performance for that length of time.

On January 30, 1962, while performing at the State Fair Coliseum in Detroit, the front man on the wire faltered and the pyramid collapsed. Three men fell to the ground, which left the rear anchorman alone standing on the wire. Karl and his brother, Herman, fell to the wire from the second level. The girl at the top level landed on Karl, and he miraculously held her until a makeshift net could be held beneath her. Two of the three men who fell to earth died that night. The third, Karl's son Mario, survived, though he is paralyzed from the waist down. The girl suffered a concussion. Karl's injuries included a cracked pelvis and a double hernia. In the midst of such a great tragedy, the Wallendas exhibited "the show must go on" tradition in the highest possible manner by performing the very next evening!

"I feel like a dead man on the ground," Karl told his wife. "I can handle the grief better from up there. The wire is my life. We owe it to those who died to keep going." The Seven was only done again on two subsequent occasions: In 1963, to prove that life does continue and that disaster does not have to end in defeat, and again in 1977, recreated primarily by Karl's grandchildren for the movie *The Great Wallendas*.

In 1998, the current generation of the Wallendas reunited the performing family members to recreate their crowning achievement, the 7-person pyramid, and reestablish their legacy in circus history. To debut the intricate maneuver, the Wallendas premiered their feat for the Hamid Circus Royale during the 1998 Moslem Temple Shrine Circus in Detroit, which was the sight of the Wallendas greatest tragedy 36 years before. It was a success.

Several attempts have been made by others to perform this intricate pyramid. None, as of yet, have succeeded in accomplishing the feat the way it was performed by the

Wallendas, incorporating the chair and without the use of nets or safety devices of any kind.

On February 20, 2001, the Wallendas once again accomplished a trick never before attempted. For the cameras of Fox TV's Guinness Records Primetime, the Wallendas assembled an **8-Person, 3-Level Pyramid**. To secure their record, they added 2 more family members to form the first and only **10-Person Pyramid!**

I can think of no greater example in demonstrating the importance of believing in each other in a team situation than that of the Wallendas. Through triumph, failure, and death the show goes on. It goes on for one simple reason—they believe in each other, emphatically.

I salute them for their accomplishments and for the example they set in believing. This level of believing has brought them worldwide fame and world-class records.

**Nothing stops the man who is a believer;
every obstacle is simply a challenge
in developing achievement.**

Chapter Two

Surround Yourself With Excellence

*"We are what we repeatedly do.
Excellence, then, is not an act, but a habit"*
Aristotle

The **need for excellence** in our lives and in our leaders is paramount in our modern-day world. It has become a must for our high officials to operate with integrity to forge into the future with success. Yet if any leader, no matter how excellent he is, fails to surround himself with equally excellent people, he runs the risk of potential problems. However, excellence should not be confused with perfection. Perfection is the state of something being as good as it can possibly be. Excellence is that *concentrated effort to always do your best and to never stop your endless efforts to improve.* Striving for excellence can be very motivating; striving for perfection, on the other hand, can be demoralizing, since perfection is often not attainable.

Excellence becomes a way of life and accepts no form of mediocrity. Excellence is never completely secured; it has to be continually strived for. Your character can become known as one of excellence, but you must constantly nurture it, protect it, and allow it to be put to the test. Abraham Lincoln had this to say on excellence: **"I do the very best I know how – the very best I can; and I mean to keep on doing so until the end."**

As a leader who believes in excellence, you must instill in your followers pride, vision, and the conscious effort to always do what is right, even when it is not the easiest or most comfortable thing to do. Having this distinctive quality will enable individuals to expect the best of themselves and of everyone on their team. To perform at any lower level would not be acceptable. Each of us determines our own destiny by the way we choose to live our life. The pattern we pick will determine the fulfillment we find in ourselves and in others. It must be clear to everyone that *excellence is not a skill; it is an attitude you live by.*

At times, excellence can be measured not by the position someone holds in life, but by the way he has handled the obstacles life has placed in front of him while trying to succeed. Regardless of your past, there is always room for excellence in your future; it only requires your commitment to obtain it. Excellent character may be manifested in great moments, but it is built in the small ones.

> **Small leaders talk about people,
> average leaders discuss events,
> great leaders exchange ideas.**

I like the following quote I found by an unknown author on the World Wide Web. It says a great deal about the true meaning of excellence:

> "**Excellence can be obtained if you . . .**
> - **care more than others think is wise;**
> - **risk more than others think is safe;**
> - **dream more than others think is practical;**
> - **expect more than others think is possible."**

Excellence becomes that unlimited attitude you pursue to enhance the quality of everything you do. Excellence means asking more of yourself than of others; it means expecting nothing but the best. I have found that those who strive for excellence do so by living their life by a certain standard. They accept no compromise, regardless of the temptations they face. Following are ten keys essential to building a character of excellence:

Keys to Building a Character of Excellence

1. **Trust Your Decisions** - Is confident in self. Places trust in others, perceives chosen processes as attainable and is committed to see them through to completion.
2. **Thinks Positively** - Continually has ability to be optimistic for a successful outcome. Allows no negativity to interfere with plans and goals.
3. **Remains Focused** - Works with a concentrated effort, can and will adjust vision to see things clearly. Pays attention and is an excellent listener.
4. **Is Honest** - Possesses the quality, condition, or characteristic of being fair, just, truthful, and morally upright. Is sincere and lives a life being true to everyone.

5. **Builds Own Character** - Lives by the highest of professional standards. Has distinctive qualities that reflect an upright and moral reputation.
6. **Is Committed** - Has a purpose, is willing to go above and beyond for all believed in. Is dedicated and devoted to see projects through to a successful fruition. Is loyal and faithful.
7. **Continues Learning** - Yearns for additional information and education. Is committed to always improving self. Is willing to share knowledge with others.
8. **Has Vision and Sets Goals** - Is eager to dream with an open imagination. Can take dreams, develop plans, place goals, and chase results. Is an optimist who enjoys teamwork.
9. **Is a Dedicated Worker** - Has enthusiastic energy and is wholeheartedly devoted to a goal for an intended purpose. Is a devoted person who can be counted on 100% of the time.
10. **Lives By The Golden Rule** - Sets an example by living by the rule of conduct that advises people to treat others in the same manner as they wish to be treated themselves.

Team Excellence Builds Champions

I again would like to point out to you that excellence should not be confused with perfection. As an example, let's look at former NBA player Michael Jordan. He had a premier NBA career, being named five times as the NBA's Most Valuable Player, and six times as the NBA Finals Most Valuable Player. In 1996, he was selected as one of the **"50 Greatest Players in NBA History."** He holds the record for leading the NBA in scoring (10 seasons), and the NBA record for the most consecutive games scoring in double digits (842 games). These are just a few of his basketball accomplishments. If you care to take the time, you will find pages and pages of his records on the internet.

I can think of no better example than ***Michael Jordan*** when it comes to referring to an excellent basketball player. He was tremendous. Yet, as good as he was, he was not perfect. He did not make every free throw, or every shot. He occasionally even got into foul trouble. Perfection was not what he was looking for, as it was not attainable no matter how good he was. Excellence was what he was chasing - to do his very best and to continually improve himself as a player and as a leader.

His excellent abilities inspired others on the team to excel. Only functioning as a team could Michael Jordan and his teammates accomplish their most prized goal—an NBA Championship. The Chicago Bulls are six-time World Champions, and they did it over an eight-year period between 1991 and 1998. **Every player on the team had to feel as though he was surrounded by excellence.** Each player was a contributor, and his focus was on excellence. Their excellence took them to Championship status.

Excellence in workforce teams is much the same in the business world. Superior companies maintain an attitude of excellence for themselves. They also strive to find customers who demand excellence within their own companies. Part of providing exceptional products and services involves a continued commitment to always strive to do better. Only through a persistent, unrelenting, steadfast search to look for new ways to improve will excellence be maintained.

Research and development is your springboard, as continuous, ongoing progress literally assures you there is no limit to what you can accomplish. If you do not keep up with the fast-paced, rapidly changing world of today, your excellence will be lost to a lack of modernizing. If you want to keep your game at the top of excellence, you must be willing to study, adjust, and advance. To achieve and maintain excellence, quit doing less than excellent work. Live by a standard of performing only at the top of your game and of always doing your best.

What the Mind of Man Can Conceive and Believe, It Can Achieve

Think and Grow Rich is the most famous work of author Napoleon Hill. It is one of the best-selling books of all time. In it, Hill has this to say about excellence*: "It has always been my belief that a man should do his best, regardless of how much he receives for his services, or the number of people he may be servicing or the class of people served."* Another one of Hill's hallmark expressions is a great way to consider excellence: *"What the mind of man can conceive and believe, it can achieve."*

Excellence is achievable by anyone who desires it, and it only takes a commitment by an individual or a team to make it happen.

Individual Excellence – Achieving the Perfect 10

In the Olympics, occasionally an individual competing in gymnastics will be given a score of 10. This indeed is rare, but when it happens it is considered to be a perfect performance. The important point to remember here is the individual's particular performance was perfect, not the athlete. However, it is accomplished because of the focused, excellent athletic ability of the athlete. Any person achieving the remarkable feat of earning a perfect 10 must be held in the highest of regard for their commitment to excellence.

Nadia Elena Comaneci is a Romanian gymnast, winner of five Olympic gold medals, and the first to be awarded a perfect score of 10 in an Olympic gymnastic event. To give you an idea of how rare a perfect 10 is, at the Montreal Olympics in the Summer of 1976, the scoreboards were not equipped to display scores of 10.0—Nadia's perfect marks were reported on the boards as 1.00 instead. She is one of the most well-known gymnasts in the world. In 2005, Fox.com selected the **"Greatest Athletes in 150 years of Sports History."** Nadia placed 4th in the final voting, ahead of Pelé and Mohammad Ali, and she was the highest-ranked female athlete. I'm sure there are many reasons why she excelled, but I have to believe the most important factor was her commitment to excellence. Isn't it amazing that in her quest for excellence, she occasionally found perfection along the way.

At the age of only 14, Nadia made history with the first perfect 10 in the Olympics. She went on to repeat the feat six times, and the world became utterly enchanted by the solemn, dark-haired Romanian who was still so young she carried a doll with her everywhere she went. Her commitment to excellence broke the barrier of achieving perfection in Olympic competition. She opened the door and proved it could be done.

Since her amazing performance, a few others have followed her example of excellence that leads to a perfected performance, but it is so rare. It only happens with those few individuals who hold themselves responsible to perform at a higher standard than anybody expects. What a perfect way to autograph your work through excellence . . . with a perfect 10.

Confucius had this to say, **"The will to win, the desire to succeed, the urge to reach your full potential... these are the keys that will unlock the door to personal excellence."**

The people, teams, and companies who survive the longest are the ones who work not just for growth or money but for excellence. They work to earn the respect of others and to give others the quality they are looking for—**excellence.**

The secret in finding great happiness can be found in one word—excellence. Knowing how to do something well is to enjoy it. There is always the best way of doing everything. If you build a character that represents your commitment to aspire for excellence, you are guaranteed to be happy with the results.

Excellence brings with it success. However, success has to be contained and controlled. If it is not, success can begin to remove your focus on excellence, therefore taking away what is really important in life—being trusted by and helpful to mankind.

Below is a poem by Ralph Waldo Emerson that will bring you back to reality when what you believe to be success gets out of control:

SUCCESS
by Ralph Waldo Emerson

To laugh often and much;
To win the respect of intelligent people
and the affection of children;

To earn the appreciation of honest critics
and endure the betrayal of false friends;

To appreciate beauty;
To find the best in others;

**To leave the world a bit better,
whether it be a healthy child, a garden
patch, or a redeemed social condition;**

**To know even one life has breathed
easier because you have lived;
This is to have succeeded.**

Excellence is the plateau of quality in excelling. It is the accomplishment of doing well to the highest degree. To have the word **"excellence"** associated with their names is the distinguishing characteristic many organizations and schools value most. It is a classification of superiority or eminence that sets you above others and in a position others will try to emulate. Excellence sets a better example than mediocrity because mediocrity is found everywhere. The profound example of excellence is found only in the extraordinary; excellence in itself breeds success. The 22 Shriners Hospitals for Children have become known as **"Centers of Excellence"** for the exemplary work they do. This distinction could not be purchased or given without merit; it had to be earned. It is so important to keep this title that they will now do anything within their power to keep it because it sets them apart from the ordinary.

Vince Lombardi is one of the most successful coaches in National Football League history. Because of his excellence, his name is inscribed on the Super Bowl Trophy. Lombardi had this to say, *"The quality of a person's life is in direct proportion to their commitment to excellence, regardless of their chosen field of endeavor."* In saying this, it becomes clear that excellence is not just needed on the football field. It is needed everywhere and in every aspect of life. It has been said that losing or having setbacks in your life can be heartbreaking. Losing your sense of excellence or moral values, however, is a catastrophe.

Losing Your Sense of Excellence or Moral Values is a Catastrophe

Our world of today contains a multitude of books, training seminars, internet sites, and social activities that all promote excellence. Isn't it amazing how few live up to its high standard? I find it hard to believe how many will sacrifice their lives to a lower standard rather than insist on living a life of excellence. True excellence cannot be the exception. It is living by a prevailing attitude of excellence when doing small things, as well as complicated things. Only then will it become a habit.

Recently, my wife and I attended a dinner function with about 200 people present. It was a nice affair—a cocktail hour followed by good food and a short program—and it was attended by wonderful people. During the program, I sat looking around the room, and I thought about the many people who worked hard to put on this event. They must have put in many hours, and yet there were several small, almost insignificant details they could have improved on: table arrangement, removal of unneeded tables and chairs, proper lighting, and so on. There was nothing extremely out of place, and I may have been the only person who noticed it because I took the moment to focus in on it. However, it is these small, seemingly insignificant details that made the difference between a good event and what could have been an excellent event. The difference in what they had, and what they could have had would not have taken an extra 5% more effort. Although many people may have not noticed, their reflection on the event would have been better. I find this to be true so often; just another 5% or 10% more effort is what it takes to achieve ***excellence.***

The future of humanity will depend on our ability to instill excellence in our children. Good habits must be introduced to children at a young age by parents who will set excellent examples. Consequently, these good habits will become a way of life for our future leaders. Building excellence is the art of instilling motivation, pride, and vision while being responsible for your actions. To some, it may sound simple, but it takes a lifetime commitment. It is achievable, however, by anyone who is desirous of obtaining excellence in life.

> *"Excellence; The best we can do is size up the chances, calculate the risks involved, estimate our ability to deal with them, and then make our plans with confidence."*
> **Henry Ford**

Gary Bergenske

VISION
With the Ability
to Make It Happen

> *"All of our dreams can come true,*
> *if we have the courage to pursue them"*
> **Walt Disney**

Vision is the profound expertise to see what is invisible to most. Good leaders have vision and create vision statements in an effort to gauge how well they are doing. They are very clear in their vision, passionate to live their vision, and relentless to find a successful completion that springboards them into their next vision. **Your vision is your plan, your future, what makes you unique; it's what matters to you.** Great leaders always stretch themselves and those around them to continually chase their dreams and visions. The essence of leadership is that you must have vision. People are inclined to be drawn to leaders that strongly believe in their own visions. Great leaders have an ability to get others excited, and in doing so bring out the best in them. This, in turn, will get their followers to aspire to dream and will help them with their own aspirations of setting personal visions.

Helen Keller—an American author, activist, and lecturer who was deaf and blind since the age of 19 months—had this to say, *"The most pathetic person in the world is someone who has sight, but has no vision."* She set an example during her 88 years of life that vision can be accomplished by everyone, even those who face overwhelming challenges in their lives. She proved visions are an important part of anyone's life who is a dreamer and expects results. Helen Keller met every U.S. President from Grover Cleveland to Lyndon B. Johnson. On September 14, 1964, President Johnson awarded Helen Keller the Presidential Medal of Freedom, one of the United States' top two highest civilian honors, for her dedicated work for humanity. I can think of no greater example or inspiration showing the results of having a vision as a part of your life. Every leader needs a vision for himself and his team or workforce.

Creating Your Vision – An Essential Key to Leadership

Creating your vision is the process of building a plan of where you see yourself or company in the future. A vision statement is a vivid, formulated description of a desired outcome. The words should give you a mental picture that will inspire you to your goal. This vision should see you in your **"preferred future,"** or rather a future that has you placed in what you believe to be the best possible position. In building your vision, consider your mission, beliefs, and capabilities.

Sit down and describe on paper where you want to see yourself in the future. Be specific, positive, and open-minded. Don't assume everything has to work within the same framework it is confined to today. Think out of the box; look at new trends, techniques, and possibilities. By writing these ideas down on paper with a desired outcome, along with a completion date, they become more realistic. Don't be afraid to write down items that might seem out of reach for the moment. Give them the opportunity to grow. Vision statements should look out five to ten years, and in some cases even longer.

Imagination Is More Powerful than Knowledge

Your vision must include your beliefs and be inspired by your imagination. Albert Einstein said, "Imagination is more powerful than knowledge." Use your imagination as you look at your goals, values, and expectations when setting your vision. As a leader, sharing your vision helps you to grow as the person in charge. Be precise, yet practical, when looking for future results. Know the players who will have to be involved to make this vision possible, and get their commitment. By using their knowledge, philosophies, and ideas, they to will take ownership in the vision. The more people who have belief in the vision, the better the rate of success, as vision provides direction.

Come up with a powerful, memorable phrase that summarizes your vision and use it in the first paragraph of your vision statement. A simple, memorable phrase can boost the effectiveness of your vision statement by keeping it on people's minds. This phrase will serve as the catalyst to keep your vision in the forefront of all involved. Often, you will not come up with this powerful phrase until the entire vision statement is written, so be patient. Taking your time will allow for the best beginning of your statement.

As the vision develops it will become a strategic plan or road map, becoming the guide for a successful run at the vision. Your leadership responsibilities will advance as others recognize your potential based on your vision and your ability to get others involved.

You will find many benefits to having a vision statement. Remember, vision statements are much longer than mission statements. Their purpose is to paint a mental picture that will get everyone on the team motivated. Make it the length that will accomplish this goal. When you have a completed, written vision statement, you will find yourself working towards a specific goal or purpose. Visioning breaks you out of normal thought processes and identifies keys needed to give you specific direction. You will begin to work more efficiently, and find higher production accompanied by increased confidence. Visioning promotes interest and commitment as it *encourages creative solutions to get you to your preferred future.*

Keep in mind the purpose of your vision statement is to energize, motivate, and stimulate creativity. A vision statement is not meant to act as a measuring tool for success; that is what your objectives and goals are for. You should base your vision statement on the best possible outcome. You may even push yourself to envision results considered even better than what would be considered to be the best outcome. An old quote I have heard sums this up best, **"Shoot for the moon. Even if you miss, you will be among the stars."** Visioning allows you to be the change you want to see in the world.

Recently, I heard a story about the day Disney World opened in Orlando. It relates itself to visions and how they move into reality. Walt Disney was involved in the everyday designing and creation of the world premier theme park. However, he passed away prior to the first patron attending. On opening day, Lillian, his wife, greeted people as they entered the park for the first time. Many people said to her, "Don't you wish Walt could have seen this place?" Her answer was always the same, **"Walt saw this park long ago, it was his dream, he had a vision of exactly how it would look."**

Writing Your Vision Statement

After you have made plenty of notes and have a firm mental picture of your vision, it is time to put your vision into a final, written copy. Write it in the present tense, imagining yourself already accomplishing your dreams. Describe it as if it existed now, as if you actually could see, hear, and feel its ideal outcome. Your statement should be emotional and passionate. This will make it even more inspiring, believable, and attainable. Aim for what you could be, not for what you are. Remember, all things are possible for those who believe. We are not limited by our talents, only by our vision. To help you in writing, consider this. Close your eyes and think:

> **It is ten years from today's date.**
> **You have done fantastically. You have**
> **created a most desirable life, it's**
> **perfect. Now colorfully describe it**
> **as if you were living it today.**

As you write your vision statement, add as many details as you can. More is better, as the more details you include, the better the picture you paint. Treasure your visions. Treasure your ideas and dreams. Treasure every positive, colorful thought that stirs your mind into thinking of what can be possible. This will enable your vision to be more powerful. Soon, your vision will be an image branded into your mind for an ideal outcome. John Wooden, who is widely regarded as the greatest college basketball coach in history with his 10 NCAA National Championships while at UCLA, had this to say, ***"Don't measure yourself by what you have accomplished, but by what you should have accomplished with your ability."***

As you continue to write your vision statement, the benefits derived from putting together this action plan will become clear to you. As your pen puts your vision on paper, it will make it easier to define the goals that will help you to build and to ultimately experience your vision. You will begin to see how your advancement will be measurable based upon your realistic progress. The benefit of having it written down gives you the opportunity to evaluate your values. It makes you accountable to yourself and to anyone else who is a party to the vision. If you aspire to live your desired future, take the time to creatively write a vision statement. Then, keep it where you can retrieve it and read it regularly. Keep in mind, what you think about often has a great chance to become reality. The benefit of having a written vision statement is essential to all leaders. Another benefit is, if the vision is strong enough, a good leader can delegate its implementation to another member on the team. Leaders know where their organization is headed. By having their vision written, it becomes easier to communicate and be absorbed by others, thereby making it more attainable.

Writing a quality vision statement will focus on your core values. It will influence your creativity, originality, and passions as you see yourself accomplishing your preferred future. A powerful vision will stretch your expectations and take you out of the comfort zone. You will begin working towards reaching a point in time where the unthinkable becomes the ordinary.

Remember, the purpose of a written vision statement is to open your mind to what is possible. Begin making notes to write your vision statement now.

Vision Statement Updating- Keeping Focus On The Target

Keeping your vision statement updated is important to its effectiveness. An outdated vision statement, whether it be already reached or no longer the target, loses any possible usefulness. Although they usually focus on the long term and do not need to be reviewed as often as mission statements, they should be looked at once a month or at least once each quarter. Reviewing them usually adds the benefit of rejuvenating your inspiration to see them through to fruition. Vision statements often generally stay the same, only occasionally needing fine tuning. However, it is not unheard of to see vision statements thrown out, only to start over again with renewed focus and creativity. At all times it should describe the hopes and dreams that give you a sense of achievement, of fulfillment, and of what you perceive to be your preferred future. We are not limited by our abilities, but by our visions. Mark Twain said, *"I can teach anybody how to get what they want out of life. The problem is that I can't find anybody who can tell me what they want."*

As good as this sounds, you need to be aware of vision killers. If you are not aware and prepared for these, you may be knocked off track. A few of the significantly great vision killers include tradition, fear of ridicule, complacency, and fatigued leaders. Then, there are always the "naysayers" who have no future and find fault in everything. Visionary minds see past these obstacles and march into the future. Vision without action is hopeless. Action without vision is only spinning your wheels. Only when you put action and vision together do you see positive results. Don't allow vision killers to hinder your plan. A good leader has the vision and conviction to see past potential problems. He inspires others with the energy to get it done. Often, people buy into the leader prior to buying into the vision. The essence of a good leader is having vision beyond the problems or challenges and being able to see the big picture.

Visions Multiply Your Future Successful Results

Visioning is an ongoing process. At no time should a vision be the ultimate goal, as there is always something beyond your current vision that will springboard you forward into the next exciting, preferred dream. Look at the automobile industry. Its visions in the 1960's of what a car should be like in the 1970's are considered to be only a stepping stone of the products we see today. There was no way to go from a car of the '60s to the computerized, digital, high-bred automobiles of today without all of the visionary people and their thought processes in between. This is true of any successful person, team, or company. Visioning is attainable, and then must progress to the next step. Each new vision requires a sense of urgency, development, and communication to others, followed by its empowerment to realization.

Thomas Edison, a visionary inventor whose fame was so widespread due to his 1093 patents, was named as **"The Greatest Living American"** in 1922 by the New York Times. His visionary attitude allowed him to invent such items as the light bulb and the phonograph. Today, nearly a century later, many of his inventions are still used, although not in the same form as they were originally. Other visionary individuals, through their own visions, have taken his original inventions and advanced them through time with modern-day technology to surpass even what Edison had imagined. It should be clear there is no end to visioning; it is wholly up to the individual mind to keep it going. The expansiveness of one's visions indicates with absolute clarity what one is committed to.

Another excellent example of how visioning can grow is revealed in the story of the Shriners of North America. In 1872, thirteen Master Masons gathered together in New York City to form the Ancient Arabic Order of the Nobles of the Mystic Shrine for the sole purpose of having fun together. Fun they had, as they drafted ritual work, designed colorful costumes, and wore the red fez. For fifty years, their fun flourished. By the year 1921, the original thirteen members grew to over a half million. The Shriners next great vision appeared as they saw themselves having a purpose, a *Shrine Philanthropy*, along with all their fun. They focused on a purpose of helping children. It became their vision to build a hospital that would provide medical care for crippled children, a task they would provide at no charge. In 1922, the first of their network of hospitals opened in Shreveport, Louisiana.

Today, the **Shriners Hospitals for Children** network is comprised of 22 hospitals in the United States, Canada, and Mexico with a 2008 budget of $826 million. For nearly 85 years, Shriners Hospitals for Children have provided some of the best medical care in the world, totally free of charge, to more than 835,000 children with orthopedic conditions, burn injuries of all degrees, spinal cord injuries, and cleft lip and palate conditions. Who could have imagined this phenomenal organization referred to as **"The World's Greatest Philanthropy"** would have developed from thirteen men's vision to have fun? It did not happen by accident; it cumulated to its current status because of the increasing visions of hundreds of men over one hundred thirty five years. This is vision sequencing. Visioning—it can take you to places never originally considered if you allow your imagination to continually grow. Vision without action is merely a dream. Vision with action can change the world.

"You are not here merely to make a living.

*You are here in order to enable the world
to live more amply, with greater vision,
with a finer spirit of hope and achievement.*

*You are here to enrich the world, and you
impoverish yourself if you forget the errand."*

Woodrow Wilson

Campaign To Be A Better Leader

Chapter Four

Organizing the Mission and Chasing the Goal

"Though we march to the music of our time, our mission is timeless."
Bill Clinton

Often people mistake a vision statement for a mission statement. A statement of vision explains where you would like to be in the future, five or ten years down the road, as we discussed in the previous chapter. A mission statement, on the other hand, gives purpose for today and describes how you will achieve your vision. A mission statement serves as your guide as to how and what is expected from you or your organization. It defines what you are all about and how you want others to perceive you. One definition of "mission" in the dictionary is: purpose, reason for being; also, an inner calling to pursue activity or perform a service. **Mission is the now, vision is the future.** It is not wise to have them resemble each other. Don't let the two confuse you; they are two different animals, each with their own distinguishable purpose.

You might ask yourself which comes first—the mission statement or the vision statement? In the beginning of a project, venture, or new company, usually the vision comes first. The vision is where you want to be; the mission, along with a strategic plan, will become the commitment or plan as to how you will accomplish the vision. A mission statement provides a course of action built on your values that will set the route to achieve your vision. At times, the strategic plan and mission have to be adjusted to align with goals that will ultimately lead to the vision. Mission statements require constant review to check their alignment with current goals, trends, and obstacles.

Ask Yourself—Do You Need a Mission?

Every person who achieves above the ordinary is on a mission, and usually it is written in the form of a mission statement. Of course, the answer depends on whether or not the statement you compose has substantial meaning to you and others on your team. If it carries no weight or meaning, it becomes just another fruitless activity of insignificant, unneeded mumbo jumbo. If it contains a worthy, credible plan of action, it will guide you and your company through the good times as well as the bad. A meaningful mission built on values and goals will carry great weight and become invaluable to your mission for success. In my mind, the most important thing about having a mission statement is having one that is meaningful, as well as attainable. So, focus on your goals, make your plans, set some deadlines, and write your mission statement. Then, carry it out with confidence, persistence, and passion, regardless of what others say or the obstacles you may run into. A key to becoming a great leader includes operating with a sense of mission in all you do.

As mentioned earlier, a vision statement may be lengthy. That is not the case with a mission statement; it should be short and to the point. It should contain the core meaning and be a summarized description of an entity's purpose. Some mission statements are only one or two sentences. They are specifically designed by some companies that way so they are easy to remember. A mission statement, at times, can be the slogan of the company. When preparing a mission statement, think carefully of how you can address the needed information in the least amount of words. The statement should be a clear representation of your purpose for existence. Remember, preparing a mission statement emanates your dreams and desired future into an organized reality. Research of other company's statements and looking for meaningful words is paramount. A good mission statement should be compelling, exciting, and passionate. Below are important factors to consider when writing a mission statement. Focus on using those that apply. This is only a check list.

10 Keys In Preparing Your Mission Statement

- **Goals**
- **Quality**
- **Excellence**
- **Consistency**
- **Service Level**
- **Product Name**
- **Values / Image**
- **Distribution Area**
- **Commitment to Clients**
- **Community Acceptance**

A sample mission statement of a moving company might be: **"Our mission is to provide a cost effective, safe, stress free move of your prized possessions to your new home anywhere in the world with professional service."** This is a one line, to-the-point statement that will keep the employees of this moving company focused. In addition, it is easy to remember and sets the tone of what the consumer can expect when hiring this company. Short mission statements can become memorable; this can make them more effective when used in a sales campaign. Other short mission statements belonging to large companies are as follows:

"To make people happy"
Walt Disney

*"To give the ordinary folk the chance to
Buy the same thing as rich people"*
Walmart

"To give unlimited opportunity to women"
Mary Kay

*"To organize the world's information and
make it universally accessible and useful"*
Google

*"To deliver sovereign options for the defense
Of the United States of America and its
Global interests – to fly and flight in
Air, Space, and Cyberspace."*
United States Air Force

"We are a global, diverse family with a proud Heritage, passionately committed to providing Outstanding products and services"
Ford Motor Company

"To solve unsolved problems innovatively"
3M

"To experience the emotion of competition, Winning and crushing competitors"
Nike

"At MonaVie, our mission is to change and improve lives around the world by introducing unique nutritional products, offering a rewarding business opportunity, and by giving back through our charitable initiatives."
MonaVie

One of the most difficult things for many people is to sit down and write a mission statement that is concise, to the point, and that says all they want it to about themselves or their company. In order to have your mission statement become really effective, it is paramount you explore all avenues and take the time required to develop one of grand scale. Your statement should reach out and grab people. The reason many never write a mission statement is they refuse to define their goals. By not accepting the responsibility to define them, they therefore have little to believe in and no realistic way to measure their accomplishments. Leaders, by contrast, can tell you where they are going, how they plan to get there, and who will be enjoying it with them when they arrive. Ralph Waldo Emerson said, *"The world makes way for the man who knows where he is going."*

Our goals can only be reached with concise planning. This consists specifically of a mission statement, a strategic plan, and a vision. These tools must be believed in by all involved and vigorously acted upon for success. By having all of the members believing, each will take ownership, therefore bringing triumph even closer. Your successes will begin to flourish the moment you start moving towards a worthwhile goal.

One approach is to look at your goals, both short term and long term. Then, evaluate what it will take to successfully fulfill your goals to, in turn, dictate your mission. Keep in mind, the main thing is there are many unique ways to build your mission statement. You should feel free and confident to do it your own way. There is no set formula or set of rules. An effective mission statement should be able to tell your company story in two to four sentences. Take your time and make it good. Get input from many members of your team or organization. Let the ideas flow. Following are 10 helpful guidelines to help you compose your mission statement:

10 Keys In Writing Your Mission Statement

- **Crystal Clear, Vivid**
- **Personalize it to You**
- **Believe What it Says**
- **Realistic / Memorable**
- **Meaningful / Measurable**
- **Only 2 – 4 Sentences Long**
- **Aligns with Vision Statement**
- **Determine What You Stand For**
- **Determine Who Your Company Is**
- **Define Why You Do What You Do**

Your mission statement should represent and provide a clear statement of your purpose. Life will take on a new meaning with your relevant mission statement. Your reason for existence will take on a new enthusiasm when you have written down exactly what is needed to fulfill your mission. Clear and simple, a mission is needed to succeed; you must be devoted to your goals because it is your goals that determine what you are to become.

When your mission is revealed, it will begin to put pressures on you, igniting a burning desire filled with motivation. I have found that those who put the demand on their lives of attaining specific goals are those who will accomplish great quests. They are those successful souls who take care of the work at hand, build on their accomplishments, and above all, pride themselves in setting the example of living with a character full of integrity.

By the time you have perfected your mission statement, had it approved by all involved, and are ready to go, you will have a new zeal in the way you look at things. You will look at the world differently. Even the biggest of tasks will look manageable and achievable. Remember, a mission that contains achievable, measurable goals is a necessity for success.

In Large Organizations Mission Statements Flourish

At universities, for example, not only does the university have a mission statement, so does each department. Carried a step further, within a department they may have mission statements for individual projects. For example, in the athletic department, they will have a mission statement. Also, each particular program within the athletic department – football, basketball, baseball - usually has its own that may change from year to year. There is no limit to how many mission statements may be in a large organization. Each one helps the team to focus on their goals and the overall vision of the larger entity. People with goals succeed because they know where they are going. Mission statements allow individual departments or teams to become motivated. They are guided by a roadmap to focus on their desired results, whether it is a successful teaching experience, research, a new patent, or a National Championship.

Mission Statements Must Be Reviewed and Updated

It is essential that your mission statement be reviewed on a regular basis. Times change, competition changes, and goals change. You must adjust accordingly. It is recommended that your mission statement be reviewed monthly. Depending on the organization, you may revise it often. In other cases, it might be years before it needs an adjustment.

Bill Gates is an American entrepreneur and the founder of Microsoft. His company works to help people and businesses throughout the world realize their full potential, and he had this to say:

> "For the first 25 years of the company, it (the mission statement) was '**A personal computer on every desk and in every home.**' It was good; very rare for a company to stick with something like that for 25 years. The reason we changed it was simply that it became acceptable . . . and so we stepped back and looked at what we were trying to do with the programming model, turning the Internet into the fabric for distributed computing, getting your information to replicate in a very invisible way so that it was available to you everywhere. Thinking of this programming model spanning all the different devices, we changed to the mission statement we have now, which is '**Empowering people through**

great software anytime, any place, and on any device.'" Bill Gates

The important point is your mission statement must stay up to date with your current objectives. Every scenario has its own time when an update will be needed. As a good leader, it is your job to see that your goals are aligned with your objectives, and ultimately your overall vision. This is needed to obtain the best possible results for a successful completion that will springboard you into the next mission. Many people fail in life, not for lack of desire, talent, or brains but simply because they never organized their goals around a mission. It has been said, **"Concentrate on making your life a mission, not an intermission."** Yogi Berra, who had a 19-year career in professional baseball as a player, coach and manager, said, **"You've got to be very careful if you don't know where you are going, because you might not get there."**

NASA (National Aeronautical Space Association) took their mission so seriously they refer to their control room as **Mission Control Center**. This room, filled with controllers who are responsible for every aspect of successful aerospace flights into outer space, is a reflection of their commitment to a successful mission. During a flight, the room is filled with specialists, each responsible for their part of the mission, including even a physician who monitors the astronauts around the clock. Frank Kranz, director of the Apollo 13 mission, is famous for having said, **"Failure is not an option."** Some people already live by this motto. I believe the rest of us should do the same. Work hard, make no excuses, and have the faith that *"Failure is not an option!"*

Gary Bergenske

"Our problem is that we make the mistakes of comparing ourselves with other people. You are not inferior or superior to any human being...

You do not determine success by comparing to others, rather you determine your success by comparing your accomplishments to your capabilities.

You are "number one" when you do the best you can with what you have."

Zig Ziglar

Campaign To Be A Better Leader

Chapter Five

Leaders Know How to COACH

"Coaching and Mentoring are both processes that bring out the best in people, allowing them to accomplish their full potential."
Gary Bergenske

The **ability of a leader to coach** his or her team is an essential key for success in any setting. Whether it be in the sports world or the business world, having the ability to inspire individuals to achieve their personal best and to play as a team builds winners. A good leader will coach others using a variety of methods to stimulate and motivate them to set goals and then achieve them. Keep in mind, authority itself does not make you a leader; it gives you the opportunity to be one. Good coaches get average people to accomplish the extraordinary.

Vince Lombardi, famed coach of the Green Bay Packers, ranks as one of the greatest coaches of all time by winning 2 Super Bowls and 5 NFL Championships. He once said this, **"A man can be as great as he wants to be. If you believe in yourself and have the courage, the determination, the dedication, the competitive drive and if you are willing to sacrifice the little things in life and pay the price for the things that are worthwhile, it can be done."**

This great quote from Lombardi applies to all aspects of life and plainly says to give up the little things, for what matters is the big things in life. Coach Lombardi also said, **"If winning isn't everything, why do they keep score."** They do because it's important to know where you are, how you measure up to others, and what you have to do to improve or win.

As printed in my previous book, ***Campaign for a Better Life***, performing as a great coach requires unconditional commitment to your team. Today, someone who leads in the business world can be viewed as a coach within his or her area of expertise. Being a coach in the workplace puts you in the position of helping others achieve their personal best. Coaches must not only teach but also lead, inspire, and motivate the group to become a cohesive unit in order for the team to perform at a high level. Coaching is a full-time job, whether you are involved in a sports team, business group, or a volunteer organization.

The ability to coach others is essential to becoming a great leader. Hard work and dedication are required to inspire others to follow. I want to list some of the characteristics needed to become a good coach within your area of expertise:

- **Be Persistent**
- **Communicate**
- **Be Committed**

- **Believe in Others**
- **Empower Others**
- **Motivate & Inspire**
- **Be a Good Listener**
- **Coach, Don't Control**
- **Guide to Independence**
- **Be Understanding of Others**

To be a good leader, you have to understand the meaning of the word "limitation." As a coach, you must have the ability to adjust and place individuals into positions that will stretch them, but not embarrass them. When you accomplish this, you will begin maximizing your coaching skills. True coaching is taking an individual to a level he can't reach alone. Most people who have never been coached will never reach their maximum potential. Coaching will develop leadership skills, build character, and clarify your core values, thereby making you a better person. Coach Lou Holtz is a former NCAA football head coach, and is currently an author, motivational speaker, and works as a college football analyst for the cable network, ESPN. He had this to say, **"Life is ten percent what happens to you and 90 percent how you respond to it."**

Coaching in the business world has been taking on a new meaning. Companies strive to get the best out of their employees by providing seminars and coaching clinics to develop people's skills and increase their productivity. To inspire employees, a good work place coach takes on the role of therapist, consultant, and confidant, as well as leader. Coaching certainly helps to reinforce your sense of self-worth, also allowing you to concentrate on your goals, and ultimately making it possible to operate at the top of your game. You might ask yourself, "Who wants a coach in the work environment?" The answer is,

"Winners who want the best out of life, and any organization that wants to go beyond where it would normally be." Effective leaders find their way, others find an excuse.

A coach earns the respect and trust of those he instructs, trains, and directs. As a trusted advisor, the coach becomes a consultant and/or counselor. Reaching the status of **"Trusted Advisor"** puts the coach in an exalted position in which he is regarded as a true leader and guide. In this position, the coach trains those under him to focus on improving themselves, not to focus on their competition. It is believed if you do your personal best, and each team member does the same, then your combined strengths will take care of the competition naturally.

This strengthens the relationship between the coach and the individual, which, in turn, causes the individual to be more invested in the group. A coach is always truthful. He instructs from knowledge and prior proven personal experiences that will build solid relationships. Coaches who have done tremendous jobs take special interest in individual's personal performances, pushing them to be their best. This, in turn, spreads into the entire team or group. Emotions and commitments are cultivated, providing outstanding results and winners. It seems to me that the coaches who concentrate on improving an individual's performance are the ones who receive extraordinary results. Keep in mind that you listen to the advice of people you trust and respsect; so, if you want your team to listen to you, give them every reason to trust and respect you. If you do this, you will become a trusted advisor, giving you the opportunity to see incredible results as you develop as a coach and leader.

Choosing a Coach

Coaches in life are selected by the proven skills they have in given arenas. If you are looking for a coach in a specific area, it is imperative to match up with someone who not only is an authority in his area of expertise, but one who will fit in with you or the group you are selecting him or her to coach. Successful companies spend big money hiring coaches to train and inspire their employees. Just as a school would hire a football coach they believe will make their team better, so must companies hire coaches in their given area of expertise, such as business, sales, technical, human resources, etc. These coaches can be occasional visitors for seminars, or full time leaders within the organization. Either way, coaching will take you to the next plateau. Successful leaders realize this and promote the coaching of team members to bring out the personal best in each.

Selecting the right person for the right job is a huge part of choosing a coach. Effective coaching can take place in the classroom, on the field, or in a boardroom. Coaching has no boundaries as to where it can take place; its limits are boundless. A good coach must be able to give constructive criticism without causing resentment and to work within his personal area of competence. His agenda has to be pure, and his goal set on improvement. A coach changes the way things look, creating an inspiring environment of achievement within the team. Vince Lombardi once said, **"Coaches who can outline plays on a blackboard are a dime a dozen. The ones who win get inside their players and motivate."** Great leaders have the ability to coach, the ability to recognize great coaches, and the wherewithal to bring these two abilities together for the betterment of the team. Over the years I have known men and women who, at times even unknown to themselves, are coaching others. This is a great quality found in leaders who aspire to help others.

Recent studies show counseling and/or executive coaching to be the most effective means for achieving measurable growth and development in individuals, groups, and organizations. The

Washington Post says, "...in the next few years, coaching will become the norm in the business world." According to Fortune Magazine, "Today's managers, professionals and entrepreneurs are hiring coaches to help them with time management, a change in career or balancing their work and personal lives." Great coaches have the capacity to inspire others with a glance. Coaching can certainly help you to attain your personal best.

Mentoring—The Art Of Helping Others

Another approach to coaching encompasses finding mentors who make personal contact with others within the organization to guide and assist them. A mentor's role is similar to that of a coach's; however, the coach is usually involved with a group or team. Mentors, on the other hand, usually work one-on-one, with the more experienced mentor guiding a new colleague or protégé along the way. Mentors check progress from time to time, avail themselves to instruct or answer questions, and help to find opportunities. A good mentor will help an individual to find success.

Mentors are found in civic, church, and fraternal organizations as well as in the business world. Organizations use mentors to help in the orientation of new members. A good mentoring relationship will build a comfort zone and set good examples for the new associate, making him eager to become involved in new activities. Mentoring focuses on the individual and thereby enhances morale, motivation, and participation in organizational programs.

Although mentoring has been coming into its own in the business world the past few years, it has been around for centuries. The word itself was inspired by the character of Mentor in Homer's *Odyssey*. In the story, Mentor is an ineffective old man. Athena, the goddess, takes on his appearance in order to guide the young Telemachus during his difficult times. Throughout the years of history, famous mentor-protégé match-ups include:

- **Socrates and Plato**
- **Plato and Aristotle**
- **Aristotle and Alexander the Great**
- **Andrew Carnegie and Napoleon Hill**

Today in the workplace, mentoring is used to groom employees who are deemed to have the potential to be a leader within the organization in the future. The employee, or protégé, is paired up with a senior level leader who will begin coaching him for a future position. Sometimes it is called shadowing if they are mentoring for a specific job. Other times, if the employee is being groomed for a managerial position, he may spend small amounts of time in many different areas of the company in an effort to familiarize himself with the overall structure of the organization. This allows the protégé to learn about the company's methods, principals, and values quickly under the direction and supervision of the mentor or trusted senior advisor.

Successful pairing up of the two is important. The mentor must be knowledgeable, informative, and motivating, yet understanding, giving the protégé the needed time to learn and fit in. The mentor is required to be confident in his own abilities and sincerely interested in someone else's growth. This guidance is not done for personal gain. It is imperative the mentor allow the protégé time not to just learn, but to absorb information, as it will prove more beneficial down the road and provide better leadership results. Mentors receive the reward of self-satisfaction for sharing their experiences to help others. Mentoring stimulates individual growth and development by helping others. A successful mentor should have the following qualities:

- **Has Knowledge**
- **A Good Listener**
- **A Positive Person**
- **Has Time Needed**
- **Adapts to Change**
- **Experienced Leader**
- **Takes Interest in Others**
- **Can Stimulate & Motivate**
- **Is Willing to Help & Facilitate**
- **Believes in Goals & Strategies**

In an effort to be helpful, some mentors go too far. It is imperative you give others the chance to learn and to become involved as you guide them. You cannot afford to damage the relationship by hurrying it along, or by over instructing, causing resentment or separation. This developmental process takes people who are willing to listen and help their colleagues. Remember, one of the most valuable assets someone's career can have is a good mentor. If you are assigned that duty, you must perform in high fashion as you take the protégé on this journey.

In the volunteer world of churches, civic groups and fraternal organizations, mentoring takes on the important role of helping to orientate new members. Mentoring becomes an essential link in getting new members involved in a position they enjoy and to keep them returning. It is important to get them into the mix of things in order to pique their interest. There are no paychecks to keep them coming back in a volunteer organization; they only come back if it's enjoyable. This is why *mentors are so important* in these organizations. They must be sure to keep in contact with the new members to answer questions, to keep them informed, and to make them comfortable. Mentors should make them feel as though they are not on their own, but rather a part of the group. Simply just being available for a phone call, advice, guidance and a laugh or two can keep someone coming back. Mentoring is encouraging, supporting, and helping them to keep going, and also helping them to deal with problems. If done properly, before you know it your protégé will become a mentor for some other new member.

In reality, we all have had mentors and coaches in our lives in some form or fashion. Both coaching and mentoring enable individuals and groups to achieve their full potential in due time. I'm sure each of us can think of someone who made a difference in the way we turned out. We are better for having learned from others. Now, as people who desire to be leaders, coaching becomes an essential key to our development and to the development of our followers. Your concentrated effort on improving yourself and those around you will build the 12 essential keys for leadership.

Gary Bergenske

Campaign To Be A Better Leader

Chapter Six

COMMUNICATING for Positive Results

"You can have brilliant ideas, but if you can't get them across, your ideas won't get you anywhere."
Lee Iacocca

C**ommunicating** is the art of exchanging information with others. It is the ability to convey ideas and feelings to another person or group through a multitude of available vehicles such as speech, writing, or body language. To properly communicate, you must be understood. This requires taking into account who you are communicating to, their knowledge of the subject, your capacity to listen, and your ability to convey your message clearly. George Bernard Shaw said, **"The problem with communication... is the** *illusion* **that it has been**

accomplished." Real leaders recognize the value of effective communicating, and concentrate on using all applications in the treasure chest of understanding one another.

A friend told me he has heard a story of mine several times, and asked why I tell it differently on every occasion. I replied to him, "I tell it the same way, but each time you hear it you pay attention to different parts depending on what you are listening to, and your frame of mind." This was an important lesson to me, as I realized a message has to go beyond your own understanding. You must be aware that what you are communicating may not be what others are hearing. To be a successful communicator, it matters not what you say, but what others hear; for what they hear, in their mind, is what they believe you said.

Miscommunication happens more often than most of us would like to admit. Just when you think you are communicating well, someone will say to you, "I'm sorry, I thought you meant…" or "All this time, I thought you were talking about this, not that." Knowing communication is so complicated, and can be so difficult to accomplish, it is truly amazing we achieve as much as we do. Keep in mind - great leaders are good communicators because they are determined to be so. They plan carefully, deliver their message with clarity, and pay attention to their audience. Below are excellent tips for communicating, and being understood:

Guidelines for Effective Speaking Communications

- **Brevity**
- **Tonality**
- **Be Clear**
- **Be Sincere**
- **Good Content**

- **Keep It Simple**
- **Answer Questions**
- **Good Body Language**
- **Speak From the Heart**
- **Understand Who Is Listening**

To communicate effectively, it is essential we realize that all people are different, as individuals and in his or her own perception the world as a whole. To be a good communicator, you must focus on others. There are times when you think others understand you; however, you must realize what you said is probably not what they heard, either because you did not make it clear or they misunderstood. Excellent communicators know how to listen, observe, and measure how clearly they are communicating.

To be a leader in today's world, it is paramount you be an effective communicator in all areas of exchanging information. It is virtually impossible to be successful without having the talent and the skills to get your message to others. For some, it comes easy. For most, these skills must be continually developed and nurtured to stay in step with the ever changing world we live in. Plain and simple - to be a leader, you must be a communicator. Knowing how to communicate is an essential key to achieving your goals with your family, friends, colleagues, and clients.

Remember, nothing is so simple it cannot be misunderstood. Richard M. Nixon, the 37th President of the United States and one of the most controversial chief executives in American history, often said, **"Let me make one thing *perfectly clear…*"** when speaking. Upon becoming involved in Watergate and resigning from the presidency on August 9, 1974, he became one of the most misunderstood presidents. His "perfectly clear" messages had become tainted and unclear.

Gary Bergenske

Listening
"When people talk, listen completely. Most people never listen."
Ernest Hemingway

The most fundamental problem in the world today is that people talk too much and listen to little. Communicating moves to the next level when you discover how to be quiet and listen. Many individuals engage their mouth prior to giving one thought about what they are going to say. It is better to think about what you are saying before you speak; when the words leave your lips, they can never be returned. The most basic way to communicate with others is to listen. In doing so, you give them your respect, attention, and show that you are considerate of their feelings.

Silence is powerful; often the need to communicate is nullified by talking too much. Ernest Hemingway said, **"When people talk, listen completely. Most people never listen."** It has been said many times - this is why we have two ears and one mouth, so we can listen twice as much as we talk. Amazingly, *silence is an art to conversation.* Below are some essential listening tips for your careful thought and review for future use:

Good Communicating Listening Tips

- **Ask Questions**
- **Be Understanding**
- **Have Compassion**
- **Capture Real Feelings**
- **Focus On the Message**
- **Ask How You Can Assist**
- **Listen More Than You Talk**
- **Encourage Others to Clarify**

Study the communication listening tips for a moment. They lead to effective communicating. There are, however, "listening busters" that will stop your communication immediately, breaking down any chance to get your message through. They include: responding too soon, talking too much, and interrupting others midstream. Do not get in the trap of judging other's ability or knowledge too quickly. It is important to hear them if you plan to have an effective exchange of information. Good listeners can become confidants, trusted advisors, and valuable leaders.

Keep in mind that wise men talk because they have something to say; fools talk because they have to say something. It is paramount in leadership roles that you become a reflection of what is acceptable and what is not. Communicating is in the forefront of how others perceive you. It is the first impression, and the most lasting impression. You must be skilled at it. Do not allow yourself to muddle up your character by not being a good listener. Think of the old cliché - **"Silence is Golden."**

Body Language

Being a great speaker with a good vocabulary is not enough when it comes to top-notch communicating. It has been proven over and over again that the biggest part of all communicating is nonverbal. What you say, coupled with how you handle yourself and how others observe you, will determine how you are perceived and received. It's what people hear that is important, not what you say. Using the right words with good delivery will have your audience's attention, but they must be able to understand your message. Be careful not to give them too much information. Keep it clean and simple. When there is a question as to what you are communicating, your actions speak louder than your words. Your character, attitude, involvement, and the atmosphere all contribute to effective communicating.

I always like to visit the room in which I will give a speech prior to the actual delivery. I try to get there, preferably before anyone arrives, when the room is quiet. I find it comforting to stand at the podium and to look all around the room, becoming familiar with it. I find out if there is a wired mike, a wireless one, or none at all. (I personally prefer a wireless.) It is reassuring to walk around the stage or the room. A calming effect emerges within you that will build stage presence. This will pay big dividends later in your body language when you make your delivery. A few minutes to acquaint yourself with the room will build confidence that transfers to positive body language. You are the message. Know your audience, be your best, and be natural but credible. Use your body effectively. This does not happen easily; it must practiced.

Having the ability to read the body language of others will assist you in becoming a better communicator. Paying attention to emotions and how others handle themselves will allow you to *"hear"* what is not being said verbally.

Improving Your Communication Skills

Proper communicating in any organization is critical. The threads of communication are interwoven through each other in the fabric of success. When properly executed, the fabric is strong, smooth, and beautiful. It only takes a few mis-communicated subjects to break down the threads, thereby causing a frayed and worn looking fabric that soon becomes only a glimmer of what it once was. Leaders within an organization must keep communications open. When they fail, they must assume the responsibility to quickly repair the message so as not to lose any of the rapport within the infrastructure. Leaders are constantly considering new ways to improve communications for the betterment of everyone around them. It must become a natural way of life.

Remember, ways to communicate are rapidly changing. To improve your communications skills you will be required to be flexible enough to accept change, and to be diligent enough to continually study and practice ways to better exchange information. I have collected some thoughts on improving my own communicating skills I believe will help me to convey my message, and will allow me to be understood more often. I would like to share them with you;

10 Ways to Improve Communication Skills

- **Listen Without Judging**
- **Think Before You Respond**
- **Not Sure? Have it Repeated**
- **Ask How Others Feel About...**
- **Stay Focused. No Mind Wandering**
- **Be A Polite, Sincere, Trusted Advisor**
- **Be Open Minded, Listen to Opinions**
- **Respect Your and Other's Character**
- **Listen to How You Sound, Your Tonality**
- **Be a Student of Learning Communications**

Your communicating skills will quickly diminish if you say things you do not mean, or make promises you cannot or will not fulfill. As a Leader, to be credible, you must follow through with any commitments you make to yourself or others. To be effective, it is important to build trust whether it be with your colleagues, employees, family, or personal friends.

When you feel like you have hit a wall, or have become stagnant at improving your skills in communicating, stretch yourself. As a leader you must continue to practice. Specific coaching from qualified professionals may be needed to assist you in reaching your full potential. Go for it, identify needs, and make it happen. The ability to continually improve the art of communicating is a basic requirement of all leaders. Do not underestimate the importance of communicating. Improve, improve, and then improve some more. This is done by continued practice. The results will be measurable and rewarding.

Communicating in the Future

The modernizations of communications are happening at a rapid pace. Just take a stroll though your local Best Buy or Circuit City store. You are likely to find many items you do not even know how to use or what they are for. It seems things are changing faster than we can adjust to. Recently, I purchased some leadership CD's to listen to. I was to leave in a couple of days on a long flight from Orlando to Reno and back again. I figured it would be an opportune time to listen to them. Not quite sure how I should go about it, I asked Jared, one of my sons. He told me I could either listen to them with a portable CD player, or as the directions implied, go to their website and download the files to a MP3 player for easy listening. I had neither of these pieces of equipment.

Jason, another one of my sons, then told me I didn't need any equipment because my cell phone was capable of receiving the files for listening. I only had to go to the store to buy a 1GB card to put in my phone, a set of earphones, and I'd be ready to go. So that's what I did. I then downloaded the information from their website per the enclosed directions in my computer and synced it over to my phone. Presto! I was ready to go. What is easy for the younger generations is not even thought of in the generations ahead of them. This is a testament to how fast communications are changing. No doubt by the time this book goes to print, many other new communication tools will have come along. It's happening that fast.

I would say communications are changing so fast, anything you write is likely to be outdated tomorrow. We have become an over-communicated civilization. We have become a society who looks to improve daily. So, how do you keep up with this express line of new communications? You must become a permanent student, willing to learn, change, and except the new wave of communications. This is a must if you are to survive with future generations, who are on the cutting edge of change. The way we communicate with ourselves and others will, at the end of the day, determine the quality of our lives. Keep in mind, successful leaders are great communicators who are abreast of the world around them.

Using old time basics, along with all or some of the fancy new tools, will keep you steadfast. One of the keys in communicating is sharing the feeling that every person is unique and of value. Benjamin Franklin said, **"Remember not only to say the right thing in the right place, but far more difficult still, to leave unsaid the wrong thing at the tempting moment."** Saying nothing sometimes says it best.

Plain old common sense has
a lot to do with good communicating
when used in conjunction with other
talents and skills.

Problem is, at times
common sense is not always
all that common.
Think before you speak!

Gary Bergenske

Chapter Seven

PASSION
Leads You to the Top

> *"Above all, be true to yourself,
> and if you cannot put your heart in it,
> take yourself out of it."*
> **Author Unknown**

When you study the lives and accomplishments of all great leaders, one ingredient is always found at the forefront of their success. It is neither talent, nor education; it is not position. Any of those alone will not bring the ultimate success. Being able to influence others is a key to becoming an extraordinary leader, but, again, it alone will not get the job done. There is one common denominator that is needed to align itself with one or more of the preceding capabilities to reach the highest level. The component I am speaking of is *passion*.

Those who make things happen do it with passion. Without passion in your heart, in your soul, and in what you believe, your efforts will never reach the pinnacle of achievement. It is passion, and passion alone, that will always out do talent. It is in those few and far between cases where you find people with talent and passion in their lives in which you find the exceptional, remarkable leaders who influence others by the masses.

The dictionary describes passion in part as "the intense enthusiasm for something; a keen interest in a particular subject or activity; intense or overpowering emotion such as love, joy, hatred, or anger . . ." Passion is the kind of commitment you find amongst the most accomplished of leaders in virtually every arena as they focus with an unconditional desire to succeed in their dreams.

Mario Gabriele Andretti, born in Montona d'Istria, Italy, is an Italian-American racecar driver and one of the most successful Americans in the history of auto racing. The name *Mario Andretti* has become synonymous with speed in the United States, causing him to be named the **"Driver of the Century"** by the Associated Press and RACER magazine When it comes to his success, he had this to say**, "Do it no matter what. If you believe in it, it is something very honorable. If somebody around you or your family does not understand it, then that's their problem. But if you do have a passion, an honest passion, just do it . . ."**

And "do it," he did, by becoming an icon in the racecar world. He did it . . . with *passion.*

> **But if you do have a passion,**
> **an honest passion,**
> **just do it . . .**

The way to get meaning into your life is by bringing passion into it. A great leader's influence over others will grow with passion, and will become stagnant if he or she depends on their title alone. For position alone leads no one. Even the leader will begin to slip by depending only upon position. It is enthusiastic passion that propels people to the top, creating meaning and purpose. The more emphasis we put on a vision or a goal, the more assuredly we pursue it, the better the results, and the stronger the feeling of fulfillment. Great athletes are not great because of their talent; they are great because of their *passion for the game*. This holds true to every person who aspires to succeed, for it is the hallmark of passion to attain your desired achievement.

Robert F. Kennedy, also called **RFK**, was one of two younger brothers of U.S. President John F. Kennedy and served as United States Attorney General from 1961 to 1964. He was one of President Kennedy's most trusted advisors and worked closely with the president during the Cuban Missile Crisis. His contribution to the African-American Civil Rights Movement is sometimes considered his greatest legacy. He was passionate in the way he lived his life and had this to say about America's future, **"The future does not belong to those who are content with today, apathetic toward common problems and their fellow man alike, timid and fearful in the face of bold projects and new ideas. Rather, it will belong to those who can blend passion, reason and courage in a personal commitment to the ideals of American society."**

No matter what level you lead at, passion is a requirement for triumph. Chase your passions down like they were your last meal. Only passions—extraordinary passions—can elevate you to the top. It has been said that nothing great in the world has ever been accomplished without passion.

> "... *Rather, it will belong to those who can blend passion, reason and courage in a personal commitment to the ideals of American society.*"
> **Robert F. Kennedy**

Have you ever noticed how many successful leaders talk about passion and about being passionate? There is a reason for it; working with passion in your life has a way of bringing out the best in you. Working with passion will naturally keep you motivated and driven, causing you to inspire others as you lead them. In athletics, when an entire team plays with passion, they become a unit with intense enthusiasm focused on reaching their goal. In the business world, teams who seemingly do the impossible are those who possess ability *and* passion. Education and work experience becomes inconsequential when those who work with passion lead the way. Leaders use passion to move projects forward, to build relationships, and to create enthusiasm, therefore causing their employees' work to optimize the team's efforts. Ben Franklin said, **"If passion drives you, let reason hold the reins."** It is important to never underestimate the power of passion, especially in a competitor.

Five Keys to Keep Passion Alive

1. **Stay Focused** - Keep your vision adjusted, allowing your emphasis to stay steadfast on your goal. Do not allow temporary setbacks to interfere with your positive emotions and enthusiasm that ultimately will lead to success.
2. **Be True To Yourself** - Believe in yourself, push yourself, make the commitment; then see it through to fruition with zeal and delight.

3. **Feed Off Each Other** - Become a team that motivates each other. Take the position of not allowing any team member to waver; encourage, move forward, learn, and grow together.
4. **Keep Priorities In Line** - Keep your emotions in check by keeping in mind that the truly passionate programs will out do and out last those nourished by talent or education alone. Do your best to have the greatest of all worlds - a passionate program fueled with talented, educated individuals.
5. **Do The Little Stuff** – Take baby steps, cherish the small success, compliment each other, build enthusiasm. This is what causes, and what keeps, a passionate program moving forward and becoming an unstoppable machine of unsurpassed success.

By following the above key points of keeping your passions alive, you will continue to develop and your vision of accomplishing the unthinkable will soon appear attainable. Soon, your work ethics, pleasures, and goals will become one and the same; measurable significant progress will become the norm, and nothing will seem impossible. Develop a passion for continued learning, and you will move further down the road, maintaining a positive nature others will look up to. Always remember, you have within you the power, the endurance, and the passion to accomplish your dreams; you only have to make them happen. Passion will drive you beyond the standard when coupled with commitment, allowing you to make a vision reality. Keep the fire burning, and go for it.

Theodore Roosevelt was the twenty-sixth President of the United States (1901–1909), a leader of the Republican Party, and a leader of the Progressive Movement. He was passionate in the way he lived his life. Roosevelt is most famous for his personality, his energy, his vast range of interests and achievements, his model of masculinity, and his "cowboy" persona. Because of the assassination of William McKinley, Roosevelt became the youngest president in United States history at the age of 42 (John F. Kennedy is the youngest elected president). Roosevelt lived a passionate life and had this to say:

> *"It is not the critic who counts, nor the man who points out how the strong man stumbled, or where the doer of deeds could have done them better. The credit belongs to the man who is actually in the arena, whose face is marred by dust and sweat and blood; who strives valiantly; who errs and comes short again and again; who knows great enthusiasms, great devotions; who spends himself in a worthy cause; who, at the best, knows in the end the triumph of high achievement, and who, at the worst, if he fails, at least fails while daring greatly, so that his place shall never be with those timid souls who know neither victory nor defeat."*
> **Theodore Roosevelt**

He led by example and enthusiasm in a time when communications were but a trace of what they are today. He dominated his era as he dominated conversations. The masses loved him; he proved to be a great popular idol and a great vote getter. His image stands alongside those of Washington, Jefferson, and Lincoln on Mount Rushmore. I have to believe it was his passion for life, for doing what was right, that kept him at the top. He is a true example of where passion can take you. Leading with passion is better than leading by the voice of reason. The passionless will not have a chance at changing history, for without passion there will not be enough followers.

Only passions, **GREAT passions**, can raise mankind to greatness.

Enthusiastic Leaders Perform With Passion

When you look carefully at the lives of all great leaders—those who have the greatest influence on others, those who have a way about them that makes things happen—you will find a common denominator. That common characteristic is having the treasure of living with passion and purpose. Great leaders are not great because of their talents; they are notable because of their passion. Enthusiastic leaders perform with passion. They are committed to what they are doing and are insanely self-possessed about their ability to make it happen. Passion naturally takes you and your followers out of your comfort zone, allowing you to see progress you might not otherwise see. Passion becomes the surging bullet that keeps moral, focus, and purpose in sync.

Following are ten traits of a program worked with passion:

Ten Traits of Building Passion

- **Dream It, Do It**
- **Driven for Success**
- **Insanely Confident**
- **Time is of No Concern**
- **Extremely Contagious**
- **Has a Defined Purpose**
- **Works Beyond Talents**
- **Unquestionable Belief in Self**
- **Courage to See Vision Through**
- **Determination Overrides Education**

History has shown that those leaders who are capable of surrounding themselves with other passionate people will find enormous success. Having a team of passionate people will move projects forward as the member's enthusiasm will manage themselves better than anyone else could. They only require direction from the leader because the fuel that drives them comes from within, not from without. **They live with passion!** Everyone is looking to put some additional excitement into their life. When the leader influences others by way of added delight and purpose, the payback will be followers who work with passion.

Time, effort, and restraints become of little concern as individuals push themselves to the maximum capacity with all of their mental and physical energy. A keen focus is kept, making it possible to exert all feasible strength to achieving one's purpose, whether it be an individual one or a full team effort. Everyone has within them a fire to have a purpose in life, whatever it might be. It should be our goal to find it; to keep it lit for self-satisfaction, and for the betterment of mankind.

If you have experienced real passion in your life, you know what I am talking about. It totally consumes your very being, taking you to another world composed of total commitment. If you have not ever felt the feeling of true passion, it is best described or demonstrated by observing others who have. I sit back in awe of those talented individuals who perform with talent that is driven by passion. They are the phenomenal examples that inspire the rest of us.

Pete Maravich was so passionate about basketball it consumed his life, and he became one of the best players of all time. Known as **"Pistol Pete,"** he became crazy for the game at the age of seven. Today, he is remembered for his dazzling ball-handling, incredible shooting abilities, and creative passing. He learned fundamental basketball and ball-handling drills at a very young age from his father, Coach Press Maravich. He would regularly shoot 100 free throws per night in his driveway and then sleep with the ball. Maravich is still the all-time leading NCAA scorer, averaging a staggering 44.2 points per game, without the benefit of a three-point line and excluding the records of his freshman year. This is due to the fact that when Pete was in his first year of college, the NCAA had separate freshmen and varsity basketball teams. Freshmen were not allowed to play on the varsity team. It was calculated that Maravich would have averaged 57 points per game with the benefit of a college three-point line. Astonishing? Yes! Understandable? You bet it is, when you understand what **PASSION** can do for your life.

Tiger Woods is unquestionably the best golfer on the circuit today, earning over $20 million per year on the course and another $60 million in endorsements. However, he still looks for and practices ways to improve his swing. He still wants to improve his swing. Can you imagine? Why? Because he is passionate about being the best—*the very best—he* can be, regardless of where he is today.

Passion drives you... it is much more than the excitement and enthusiasm on the surface others see. It is that burning desire buried deep down in your gut that says, "I am going to believe in myself, I'm going to do my best, and I'm going to keep on doing it till the end regardless of any pressures or what others think." If you are passionate about what matters in your life, there is no doubt you will be successful. Learn from the passionate lives of others. Do what you like, get passionate about it, get others to join your passion, and make a difference. Great leaders know the power of passion. You can, too.

Gary Bergenske

***I am going to believe in myself,
I'm going to do my best, and
I'm going to keep on doing it till the end
regardless of any pressures or what others think.***

Campaign To Be A Better Leader

Chapter Eight

PERSISTENCE
Make It Your Way of Life

*"Defeat may test you; it need not stop you.
If at first you don't succeed, try another way.
For every obstacle there is a solution.
Nothing in the world can take the place of
persistence. The greatest mistake is giving up."*
Author Unknown

Success is definitely associated with persistence. Successful people stay focused on their goals with unmatched determination. They may make mistakes, but they never quit. It has been proven over and over again - when you mix ordinary talent with exceptional perseverance, the results are an extraordinary magnitude of success. As we persist, the difficult becomes easier, not because it has changed, but because our ability has increased.

No great achievement will come to fruition without persistent work.

Hank Aaron's most notable achievement was setting the Major League Baseball record for most career home runs with 755, a record he held for 33 years until being surpassed by San Francisco Giants' outfielder Barry Bonds on August 7th, 2007. Aaron, who attributes his success to perseverance, had this to say, **"My motto was always to keep swinging. Whether I was in a slump or feeling badly or having trouble off the field, the only thing to do was keep swinging."** His determination kept him at the top of the game and put him in the record books.

Nothing could be worse than to realize you had given up to soon, only to find out later you were so close to victory. You never really know how close you are; however, through determined continuation of action and belief over a period of time, all goals begin to look attainable. The secret of success is often the constancy to purpose. **Never, Never, Never Quit!**

> **Keep in mind...**
> **Lofty goals always take time,**
> **energy, hard work, and a ton**
> **of persistence to accomplish.**

Dale Carnegie said, **"Most of the important things in the world have been accomplished by people who have kept on trying when there seemed to be no hope at all."** Getting ahead ultimately requires avid faith in yourself and your purpose. It is important to contain the determination to never allow your energy or passions to be hindered or discouraged by temporary setbacks or negative individuals. In Aesop's fable, ***The Tortoise and the Hare,*** we learned the race is won not always by the swiftest, but by the one who keeps on running. In the confrontation between stream and a rock, the stream always wins—not through strength, but by perseverance. In life, it is the *persistent* who find the rewards of success. I cannot find a better way to say this than as quoted by Calvin Coolidge, the thirtieth president of the United States.

> *"Nothing in this world can take the place of persistence. Talent will not; nothing is more common than unsuccessful people with talent. Genius will not; unrewarded genius is almost a proverb. Education will not; the world is full of educated derelicts. Persistence and determination alone are omnipotent. The slogan 'press on' has solved and always will solve the problems of the human race."*
> **Calvin Coolidge**

Just as it was when President Coolidge said it years ago, so it is today. "Persistence and determination are **_omnipotent_**," meaning invincible, unstoppable, or all powerful. As a leader, you must remember- regardless of your talents, or the talents of others, in the end it is the quality of perseverance that prevails over most any challenge. It is difficult to overcome someone who never gives up.

Keys of Persistence

- **Believes with Passion**
- **Full of Positive Energy**
- **Committed to the Task**
- **Continuance to the End**
- **Devotion to See it Happen**
- **Wholeheartedly Dedicated**

- **Never Becomes Discouraged**
- **Uses Diligent Action, Has Drive**
- **Determined and with a Purpose**
- **Continues Steadily Despite Obstacles**

Success is nearly always a reflection of one's drive and persistence. The extra energy expelled to attempt another try and the extra effort built on determination is what builds winners and great leaders. Failure is only postponed success. No is only "no for now." It is the habit of reaching beyond where the normal person can see that moves mountains. It takes courage to work out of the norm, but the rewards are great for those who dare.

Albert Einstein, who was named *"Person of the Century"* by *Time* magazine in 1999, had this to say, **"I think and think for months and years. Ninety-nine times, the conclusion is false. The hundredth time I am right."** He also said, **"It's not that I'm so smart, it's just that I stay with problems longer."** Wise words from a wise man. Great lessons can be learned from him. Persistence, the habit of never giving up, as history has proven, builds successful leaders. When you are in constant pursuit of your most personal dreams, you will expand and grow. You have to continually be looking for all the pieces of the puzzle, never knowing when the final piece will fall into place. When it does, you will have a feeling of profound accomplishment. Each time this happens, your desire to perform with persistence will escalate.

Many people limit their potential by failing to give it all they have; they give up before they should. A leader never gives in to thinking he or she is beat. If you do, you are defeated, solely because of your own thinking. You must keep on believing you will prevail. That's how men accomplish the things thought to be *"impossible"*—by sticking with them.

Remember, the impossible is accomplished everyday by someone. It's accomplished by moving forward, creating something new, or finding another way to do what was believed to be unattainable. Wealth, fame, and power are all found by the individuals who are persistent enough to find it. To succeed greatly, you must be willing to sacrifice greatly. As a Japanese proverb states, "Money grows on the trees of persistence."

Money Grows on the Trees of Persistence

Webster's Dictionary describes an individual who is persistent this way: *Tenaciously or obstinately continuing despite problems or difficulties, continues to follow the same course of action, no matter what* . . . The end product is a persistent person who continues trying and trying with unrelenting passion.

Abraham Lincoln, the 16th president of the United States, was one such individual. Today, he is regarded as one of the finest presidents in the history of the United States. His journey to reach the highest office in the land was met by many challenges and disappointments; however, his determination never wavered. Abraham Lincoln's life demonstrates great character; his leadership developed an administration that guided the country though the Civil War.

Lincoln was unwilling to let the poverty and the hardships he experienced as a child deprive him of the life he dreamed of. From an early age, he was strong-minded, despite less than one year of formal education. He schooled himself, eventually becoming a lawyer. His self-driven mission of doing his best to become a leader prepared him in 1860 to be elected to the highest office, President of the United States. His persistence had finally paid off, but not before years of work that often found him on the losing side. Lincoln's constant, faithful pursuit of achieving success is what brought him to the top.

Gary Bergenske

Abraham Lincoln's Incredible Journey to Become The 16th President Of The United States

1809 Born in one-room log cabin
1816 Worked to help support family
1818 His mother died
1831 Failed in business
1832 Defeated for legislature
1832 Lost job, denied law school
1833 Declared bankruptcy
1834 Elected for legislature
1835 Engaged to be married, fiancé dies
1836 Has a nervous breakdown
1838 Defeated for speaker of state legislature
1840 Defeated for Elector
1843 Defeated for Congress
1846 Defeated for Congress again
1848 Defeated for Congress 3rd time
1849 Rejected for Land Officer job
1850 Son dies, age 4
1851 Father dies
1854 Defeated for Senate
1856 Defeated for Vice President
1858 Defeated for Senate again
1860 **ELECTED** President of the United States

President Lincoln's path to the White House was long, taking nearly 30 years to achieve his dream. He had many opportunities to say, "I give up." That was never an option with him. Reaching his goal was what mattered.

Worthwhile goals often take more time than you plan for. Stay focused and on track. The persistent person is the one who meets the challenges, overcomes the setbacks, and finishes a winner. Abraham Lincoln was a great leader who said, **"The sense of obligation to continue is present in all of us. A duty to strive is the duty of us all. I felt a call to that duty."** Following is another quote of his to motivate you to persist until you have reached your goals:

> **The path was worn and slippery.**
> **My foot slipped from under me,**
> **knocking the other out of the way,**
> **but I recovered and said to myself,**
> **It's a slip and not a fall.**

Persistence fueled with energy will conquer all things. Even if the progress seems slow, by moving forward, it will continue. Do not become discouraged. Thomas Edison said, **"Nearly every man who develops an idea works at it up to the point it looks impossible, and then gets discouraged. That's not the place to become discouraged."**

Perseverance can take you to an enchanting place where difficulties disappear and impossibilities cease to exist. It takes dedication, hard work, and faith to make the dreams of your life become reality. Continue to think, "I may not be there yet, but I'm closer than I was yesterday." Often, it's the last key on the ring that unlocks the dead bolt and opens the door.

Many individuals fail simply because of their lack of persistence to look at challenges from another angle. Often, it takes a new plan, a lesson learned from a failed test, or the faith to try again that inches you closer to the solution. You, too, can accomplish something great and become a tremendous leader in the future. Don't allow fear of the time it will take scare you away. Time will pass, and it is up to you to make the best possible use of it. Remember, the greatest oak was once a little acorn that held its ground.

The Killers of Persistence are Fear, Doubt, Time, and Worry

Fear - The apprehension of the unknown frequently causes leaders to become more troubled than they should. Negative thoughts must be replaced with positive actions to keep the momentum.

Doubt - It is essential that uncertainty or mistrust be kept to a minimum. Skepticism is overcome by belief in one's ability to find the best in the mission and others involved.

Time - All goals are not met in the original allotted period; having the flexibility to re-adjust to a new, constructive, optimistic timetable, coupled with holding on to your vision will keep your dreams alive until success is discovered.

Worry - Do not allow anxiety to take control; it can cause great nervousness and discomfort. The proper attitude will build a cheerful, confident image that will encourage your self-esteem to the end.

As a leader, your actions and attitudes are constantly on display to others. How others perceive you, what they read into your actions, and where they feel you are headed will determine the amount of support you will receive. These small factors can become of great importance when it comes to keeping others motivated and persistent in reaching the ultimate goal, regardless of how much effort or time it takes. The following poem by William Shakespeare has great insight to this:

"Listen to many, speak to a few.
When words are scarce
they are seldom spent in vain

'Tis best to weigh the enemy
more mighty than he seems.

Wisely, and slow.
They stumble that run fast.

A friend is one that knows you as you are,
understands where you have been,
accepts what you have become,
and still, gently allows you to grow."
William Shakespeare

    The responsibility of keeping others operating at their maximum performance belongs to the accomplished leader. When this is done, persistence becomes a standard way of doing business for the individual or group you are leading. For those who learn not to quit, persistence becomes a habit. Again, as President Coolidge said, **"Persistence and determination are *omnipotent*,"** meaning, *invincible, unstoppable, or all powerful*. This is the way of life for the successful leaders who aspire to do their best, as they know no other way than to give it all they have until the end.

    Keep in mind—great leaders are measured by the performance of their followers. The art of persuasion will go a long way in influencing others to do their best. Think about how you lead. Are you using your talents in ways to motivate others to their maximum potential? If you are, the measuring stick will show the actions of your cohorts to be persistent team players who look to be lead by example. Being persistent is a 24-hours-a-day, seven-days-a-week commitment. Make your commitment, and success will follow.

Persistence

It takes a little courage
And a little self control
And some grim determination,
If you want to reach the goal.

It takes a deal of striving.
And a firm and stern-set chin,
No matter what the battle,
If you really want to win.

There's no easy path to glory,
There's no rosy road to fame.
Life, however we may view it,
Is no simple parlor game;

But its prizes call for fighting,
For endurance and for grit;
For rugged disposition
And a don't-know-when-to-quit.
Unknown

Chapter Nine

Earning Loyalty and Respect

> Talk to people in their own language. If you do it well, they'll say, *"God, he said exactly What I was thinking."* And when they begin to respect you, they'll follow you to the death.
> **Lee Iacocca**

Over the past couple of years, I learned the true meaning of loyalty and respect as I campaigned for an international office that would place me on the Board of Directors for both the Shriners of North America and the Shriners Hospitals for Children. This position requires individuals of high character, and the campaign to acquire this office is a test of one's ability to gather around him loyal followers. I was able to rank who was the most loyal to me by observing those who instilled their trust and respect in my every move. Those faithful supporters who worked till the end demonstrated to me the true meaning of loyalty. **Loyalty was not about if we won or lost; one's loyalty stays the same regardless.** It is about being true to each other no matter what the outcome. I learned the lack of loyalty is one of the foremost reasons for failure.

Losing in my first attempt at the position only made the individuals who believed in me more determined; they were loyal to see me reach my goal. Their loyalty to me became an inspiration, pushing me on to give it a try a second time. It was the respect we had for each other and the shared mission to see our goal to victory that bound us together with loyalty that made it true to the heart. The loyalty, trust, and belief between the supporters across North America flowed up and down the structured campaign plan, giving it strength. Success was to be found in the persistence of hard work, learning from our failure, and the continued faith of our loyal team.

Woodrow Wilson, the 28th President of the United States, said, **"Loyalty means nothing unless it has at its heart the absolute principle of self sacrifice."** I know this to be true by what I witnessed from those individuals who gave it their all to see me succeed. Working limitless hours, traveling without reimbursement, and arranging their schedules to meet the required dates of the campaign proved to me beyond a doubt their sacrifices equated to loyalty.

The election was held in Anaheim, California. The win itself, although a tremendous accomplishment, did not compare with the feeling of pride felt by all on the campaign team as we congratulated each other. It was the team effort that made it great, each of us taking ownership of the victory due to our hard work.

Many with tears in their eyes felt the physical sensation; but more importantly was the inner heartfelt emotion of finding success among trusted, loyal counterparts. The win created a bond whereby honesty, character, integrity, faith, love, respect, and loyalty flowed within and between the hearts of those who were committed to the end.

We all knew we had set the expectations high, and then found men and women whose integrity and core values were respected. We all worked together, getting each other's agreement on a course of action for the campaign. Then, they pledged their ultimate trust and loyalty. The result was the win. It could not have been better. It became unmistakably clear to me that what made this win a great honor was the respect and loyalty of my colleagues. **Great leaders are *"successful leaders"* for only as long as they have the respect and loyalty of their supporters.** Below are ten key characteristics of loyalty found in persons of integrity:

Ten Key Characteristics of Loyalty

- **Reliable**
- **Faithful**
- **Trustworthy**
- **Respectability**
- **Dependability**
- **Full Allegiance**
- **Feeling of Duty**
- **Earned Day by Day**
- **Devoted to a Cause**
- **Center of Human Dignity**

If a person does not respect himself, neither can he be loyal to another. You first must be true to yourself before you can move forward with a dedicated allegiance to others. A test of character is how you respect others who can be of no possible service or assistance to you. It is important to respect everyone, even if you disagree with them. Loyalty among people develops from respect, not from total agreement on every subject. **Loyalty cannot be bought. It is not for sale; it _must_ be earned**. There are no secrets or short cuts to obtaining and retaining loyalty. It is earned by perfection, persistence, hard work, understanding, and good communication with all around you.

As long as it takes to earn loyalty, it can be lost in a moment by failing to abide by the highest of moral standards. Whether you realize it or not, more often than you think someone is watching and evaluating you. How you act, how you treat others, your care and love for those you don't know tells the story of who you are. Loyalty is based on the real you, not an artificial façade. Always be your best!

In 1947, Jack "Jackie" Robinson, the first African-American major league baseball player of the modern era, faced many challenges on and off the field. While not the first African-American professional baseball player in United States history, his Major League debut with the Brooklyn Dodgers ended approximately eighty years of baseball segregation. To earn the acceptance of others, in addition to his excellent talent, his behavior had to be superb, as he was always under a microscope with tainted eyes looking at him. He handled it like a professional and said, "I'm not concerned with your liking me or disliking me… All I ask is that you respect me as a human being."

> *"I'm not concerned with your liking me or disliking me… All I ask is that you respect me as a human being."*
> **Jack "Jackie" Robinson**

His demeanor, talent, respect for others, and a positive attitude prevailed. Under the most difficult of challenges, he excelled, slowly earning the respect and loyalty he deserved. Robinson won *The Sporting News* Rookie of the Year Award and the first Major League Baseball Rookie of the Year Award. Two years later, he was awarded his first National League Most Valuable Player Award. The Baseball Hall of Fame inducted Robinson in 1962; he was a member of six World Series teams during his nine year professional career. He earned six consecutive All-Star Game nominations and won several additional awards during his career. His proficient career earned him respect due to his character, which was filled with dignity. Below are ten key factors needed in the building of your attitude, regardless of how difficult it may be at times. This will ensure others will respect your actions, thereby creating a deep loyalty to you and your efforts.

Key Attitudes that Build Loyalty

- The greatest joy - **Giving**
- The greatest asset - **Faith**
- Most satisfying work - **Charitable**
- The greatest reward - **Compliments**
- Most significant entity in life - **God**
- Most powerful energy in life - **Love**
- Most cherished possession - **Integrity**
- The best esteem builder - **Confidence**
- Most effective communication - **Prayer**
- The greatest motivator - **Encouragement**

Following these key attitudes will build loyalty in your life, and those around you will look up to you with respect. When you acknowledge people around you with a greater appreciation than you expect to receive back, you will become a person of integrity.

As with any characteristic, if you do not keep it constantly in the forefront of your behavior you will lose its benefits. Losing self respect, becoming a gossiper, using poor judgment, or having self-pity for yourself will be grounds for people to look at you in an unprofessional way. This kind of wavering behavior will break down any compulsion of loyalty they may have had for you. It cannot be stressed enough - ***loyalty has to be earned*** and can only be kept by its continual preservation.

When does loyalty become important?

You might ask yourself, "When does loyalty become important? When does it begin to make a significant impact in your life?" I would venture to say it begins as a young child. I believe to have loyal followers, loyal friends, and loyal counterparts, you must first experience being loyal to others. This process is born in the hearts and minds of our future leaders at a very young age. How their parents, grandparents, teachers, and others who have an impact on them handle respect and discipline will play a significant role in their future.

Children who learn the value of respect at a young age will find the benefits and advantages of being loyal. **Loyalty in children inspires unlimited hope.** This will be transferred into others being loyal to them in return. It is therefore earned based on exercising good core values and making sound choices, and then further developed by consistent, proper behavior. Loyalty grows, becomes stronger, and can become contagious in the inner circle of committed individuals. Living with integrity and dignity is found in those who live by the highest of standards and is more easily passed on to the next generation. These are the same parents and grandparents who give more than they receive. When spawned in young children, this type of response has the greatest chance for success.

It becomes paramount for those who are influential in the lives of our future leaders, the young children of the world, to act accordingly. Too often, those who young children are most respectful and loyal to are not living as good role models. One of the greatest responsibilities in life is to leave this world better than you received it. This starts with improving the minds and lives of the next generations, by teaching them to be respectful of and to be loyal to all. When done properly, the rewards are tremendous.

With no monetary benefit, the positive reinforcement that is encouraged through excellent behavior in our youth is compensation enough. Anyone who has worked with charitable organizations knows what I'm talking about. The feeling of helping others takes on a new dimension, unrivalled by any other form of remuneration. Teaching our future leaders to be loyal will pay big rewards in everyone's future, young and old alike.

My wife Anne and I have six children, and we have experienced the ultimate gift from them. This gift of respect and truthfulness they give to each of us and their siblings is the unwavering bond we live with. We trust we are all loyal to each other's dreams and ambitions, thereby helping each other to achieve our best, even if it knowingly requires sacrifices by ourselves and other members of the family. This motivates each to do their best. This type of behavior will be transferred to the next generation by witnessing the examples set for them in their everyday activities. The examples shown in daily life will become an understood, required way of behaving.

I cannot express enough the importance of the values we set in our children when it comes to developing loyalty and respect. It should be a dominant feature in a parent's aspiration of building a child's core values. When loyalty, respect, and trust are in place, most any crisis or predicament will work itself to an acceptable, manageable conclusion, regardless of the magnitude of the challenge. Accept no false replications; demand only the highest degree of loyalty and respect from your children. The benefits will last your lifetime.

Credibility Builds Loyalty

Leaders keep and continue to build their credibility by always doing what is right. There will be times in your life when you will be challenged to make the right choice. More often than we would like to admit, we are faced with deciding what is best for our career or what is most convenient in our life for the moment. Which do you choose? Often, the decision requires the mentally tough; those who are consistent and have their priorities in line, and who can make the correct, uncompromising choice. The alternative is taking the uncomplicated, comfortable way out. This will result not only in less productivity, but it will also begin to eat away at your credibility. Remember, you start building your credibility with your first impression the moment you meet someone. Then you never stop; you keep on adding value to your trustworthiness for the rest of your life.

Leaders who plan to grow must be committed to not only representing what is right, but to living a life of what is respectable, appropriate, and proper. Leaders also know that, through the good times and the bad, loyalty will prevail over imperfections and human errors. **Leaders know loyalty comes from the heart; it is fueled by self respect and core values.** By following this formula, your credibility will naturally push the respect others have for you to a higher plateau. This same type of behavior will assemble those around you who believe in you and your programs. Leaders who have the respect of their peers deliver more than they promise. This will warrant their loyalty, earning you a team of individuals who will give it all they have until a successful conclusion is achieved.

The great leaders of our time are masters at building their characters; they do it day by day. They are the veterans who expand with their desire to improve not only themselves but everyone around them. They do it by being problem solvers. They look at the big picture, and they give back more than they will ever receive. Ultimately, in the end, when they grow old and look back at their careers, it's the loyalty and respect of their peers and family that will mean the most. They will have achieved the highest of honors. One that is priceless - a character filled with integrity that was nurtured from making the *"right"* choices.

To close out this chapter I would like to leave you with a portion of an inspirational note I received from my Campaign Manager, Happy Schuur, after our victory in the election. Happy worked tirelessly, traveled on his own nickel, and kept me pumped up to support our effort. He would have done anything legally possible to insure a win, but it was his loyalty to me that meant the most. His short note below exemplified his loyalty:

My Good Friend Gary,

Thank you very much for letting me work with you while campaigning for the Imperial Line. I really appreciate being associated with you and "breaking bread" with you these past years. I gained a great friend in the process – YOU. No matter what all titles you got, in my book – your best title is, "My good friend, Gary."

Your Old Buddy,
Happy

Gary Bergenske

Chapter Ten

Embracing Change Builds Leaders

*"People readily accept change
When changing is less painful
Than not changing."*
Gary Bergenske

Creativeness involves breaking out of established or traditional patterns in order to look at things differently. Finding alternative solutions is essential to the survival of any organization. Some modify what they are doing in order to advance; others make adjustments when they feel the heat to do more. One thing for sure - the world around us is transforming at a rapid and record-breaking pace. In order to just keep even, you must be willing to change not only how you look at things, but how you process and respond to them.

It's never too late to become the person you have always dreamed you could be.
To do so, you must be willing to embrace change.

Too often, people resist change in their lives because they are content, or for fear they might not like the outcome. Changing is a law of life; it brings with it innovation, prosperity, and success. *Change* moves people and their organizations forward. At times, the results are not immediate, but are forthcoming with diligent work by people who believe.

Change fails when you deal with individuals who are reluctant to give up the necessary valuable assets or control needed for the transformation. People will easily tell you, "*I do not resist change,*" yet they will fight you till the end on being changed. Why? They are scared of the possible results! They are unwilling to make the sacrifices and leave their comfort zone.

To better understand why people resist change, let's look at some key reasons why most individuals fight the very thought of becoming different or working outside the norm.

Unacceptable Reasons to Not Change

- **Loss of Assets**
- **Costs Involved**
- **Potential Risks**
- **Possible Failure**
- **May Be Criticized**
- **Change in Life Style**
- **Fear / Not Organized**
- **May Not Be Comfortable**
- **Friendships Could Be Challenged**
- **Inability to Return to Pre-Changed Status**

Leaders look for change; they search for ways to improve. Leaders persuade, influence, and guide people to break out of "the box" and change. They exemplify change by acting in ways their followers can imitate. Change, or *"modernizing,"* as I like to call it, is a necessity in life; it keeps our interest and keeps us moving to new horizons. Life without change would be boring, stagnant, and unproductive. Leaders who make a difference embrace change. They have a plan and with it create change. Great leaders realize that whether they are changing or not, change is taking place in the world. It is on their personal agenda to be at the top of their game and to stay in the forefront for the best results. They know future successes are in direct proportion to their ability to modify and adjust to a more modern world as it presents itself.

The tempo of change will not be slowing down anytime soon. If technology continues at its current pace, organizations will constantly acquire unimaginable modifications, resulting in changes in every facet of life. Those individuals and companies who plan for and accept change will be those who survive as the fittest. This will open many doors for the leaders who are open-minded enough to modernize quickly to tomorrow's new standards. They will swiftly prove that success is not only determined by your ability to change, but by how fast you adapt to change.

Those leaders who are capable of modernizing more quickly than their competition will be the true winners as they satisfy customers and clients with their newly found techniques. Change will become the best friend of successful leaders as old traditions fall short of satisfying the modern day consumer. Even those considered to be the most progressive today will require continued change tomorrow to keep moving forward.

There is no question about it. Our great leaders of the future will be those gifted individuals who are talented, accomplished men and women who lead by making changes—by ***modernizing***. It then will become their mission to influence others to follow. The degree of their success will be a reflection of their ability to assist others to develop. This will provide empowerment for additional modernizing, which will in turn bring added value to the leader, allowing him and his entire team to strengthen.

The Value of Change

Leadership today is measured by the number of and value of one's new ideas. A leader can place himself ahead of the rest by being open - minded to change. He should be in pursuit of finding alternative ways of doing the same old thing, with an emphasis on providing better results. Whoever desires continuous success and growth must change. Confucius said, ***"Only the wisest and the stupidest of men never change."***

What makes change difficult is people overrate the value of what they now have, and miscalculate the value of what they could have. People seriously misjudge the significant improvements in life they could enjoy if they were only willing to make the small sacrifices change demands. If change, or modernizing, brings value, then it reinforces your accepted principles and standards of life. Change, therefore, naturally empowers you as an individual or as a group to ***GROW***. Our usefulness expands in proportion to our willingness to change. Change equals added value.

One's value as a leader will be determined not only by his or her ability to change, but by the capability to lead others through the necessary changes needed for growth within the organization. Keep in mind, all change is not growth, in the same way that all movement does not advance you. However, all change or movement does provide additional insight to a brighter tomorrow because of the added value learned. Often, the value of a second chance is brought about by having the opportunity to change. Never sell yourself short. Look for change, relate to change, and embrace the value change brings with it. History has proven that when you are through changing, you are through.

As a Leader, Do You Have the Guts to Change?

Being a leader who promotes change can be a lonely position, especially when it does not work out as well as you had hoped. There are constantly the nay sayers who proclaim to know it all and are quick to say, "*I told you so.*" They are the ones who are going nowhere; they will soon be leading no one. They create animosity. Life is accelerating past them while they live in the good old days of dying traditions and worn out customs. Our future leaders must possess a sense of urgency in seeing their dreams come true. **They have to believe being different will translate into being better.**

Leaders who have the guts to change are visionaries focused on finding new routines aimed at improving the way they lead. Successful change requires getting your team up to speed with you. They must all feel the urgency within them to get the job done in a timely fashion. As the team grows, they will energize each other. This will help bring acceptance to the change, allowing for it to do well.

Never doubt the power of groups working together on a common goal requiring change if it improves their lives. Their momentum can become unstoppable. Change can be inspiring if you can visualize the final results. A leader must be able to paint a picture of the desired goal in the minds of his team and motivate them to its conclusion. It is the leader who must orchestrate the steps needed to accomplish the goal. It is the leader who must take responsibility. Once changed, the old way becomes history.

Be the leader that has the guts, the heart, and the horsepower to lead others through change, and you will be richly rewarded for your leadership. Change makes the difference; successfully done, it brings huge credit to its leaders, adding substantial worth to their credibility. Below are 5 key tools needed in motivating people to change:

Five Key Steps to Change

1. **Should We Change** - This step evaluates where you are as you go through the gates of what change could do for you. It examines the current effects of the way procedures are carried out. A determination must be made about whether this is the correct time and place to look at change for this specific problem or area. Here you will become aware of and evaluate what sacrifices must be made to fulfill change.
2. **The Need To Change** - Here the reasons are listed as to why change is required. This is critical, since new ideas will begin to come to the surface as you anticipate how to make things better and how to bring added worth. This step will become the foundation of building the plan for executing change.
3. **Benefits Of Change** - In this phase, you will begin to see the added value a change will bring. Here momentum begins to build as the pictures are painted, and visions are seen of where you could be if you were to change. Here you should evaluate the organization's strengths and weaknesses. Begin getting others involved to get additional ideas on what the change will provide.

4. **Act On Changing** - Communication and the implementation of team building are put into action with a plan to make the change a reality. Here the leader is required to prove himself, as he must lead the team through the most difficult portion of change - making it happen while keeping others satisfied. Be prepared. Be persistent and have a passion in what you are promoting. Motivate others to act; action promotes change.
5. **Accepting The Change** - This step relates to getting everyone on board to not only accept the change, but to believe in the change. Often this step takes the longest, as some are slow to change and only admit it was best after time has proved its worthiness. Keep the momentum and continue to monitor; do not allow your progress to slip.

Change is best accomplished when an effective leader follows a specific plan to lead his organization through to the plan's acceptable completion. Attempting to change people without going through each of the steps will place the outcome at risk. When dealing with groups of people, extraordinary care must be taken not to rush past any of the key steps. Doing so will cause doubt. ***Following your plan will help to cement footsteps along the way so your intended system for achieving change will be cast in stone.*** This will give others little reason to look back and will allow them to think logically. Using good sense combined with rational behavior will motive people to move into the "acceptance" step of change with little resistance. When this is accomplished, others in the group will soon follow.

The smaller your groups are, the easier the battle of securing change. Managing one or two people during the course of change is much easier than large groups. In this situation, questions can be answered quickly, keeping the movement always going forward. It becomes more relaxed and informal; one–on-one conversation can move your coworkers through the five steps of change confidently.

Large groups, such as sizeable corporations, big cities, state government, or the national government require teams of leaders working together in mass to convince the voters to vote for change. Think of the network of teams needed to propose a change in key decisions, such as gun restrictions, medical care, or retirement issues. Although huge in scale, they must travel within the same five steps of change, cumulating with a vote in the *acceptance of change* step.

I have found that phenomenal leaders personally excel at bringing change in small groups. I have also found them to be skilled in their attention to detail and motivation to bring change in medium size groups. The few who are capable of leading the large groups through change are the ones who know how to build teams of leaders who all work together to bring about change. This is where great leaders are empowered with knowledge, managerial planning, charisma, and people skills. When properly done, this will allow the masses to see the benefits of changing, and to accept it. This is where real leaders are tested, trusted, and proven. They are driven, regardless of set backs, to find success not just to be successful, but because they believe in what they are working for.

Making Change Permanent

Tradition and old customs are formidable forces to contend with. Your efforts to manage change can falter and slither back to old habits if not carefully monitored during the early stages. To make change permanent, it is imperative to reinforce the new way of doing business with a strong, supportive plan. A new process must be refined, found to be correct, and given time to grow roots. If this final portion of the *acceptance to change* step is not seen through to the end, massive amounts of effort will have been exhausted, providing little or no benefit.

Leadership can bring about a full acceptance of change, or be responsible for allowing it to slide back. **Big changes require enormous follow up**. A good leader will be effective in cementing the change into permanent status - creating stability with *stick-ability*. This will provide for the continuance of the new procedures even after the leader has moved on. Remember, great leaders are valued by how those he has influenced perform after he is no longer there.

As we look back at this chapter, I hope you have come to better understand not only how change affects our lives, but have become aware of change and its ultimate benefits for improving life experiences. It has become clear to me; our ability to navigate within the challenges of change with a positive attitude will determine how effectual the adoption and implementation of change will be. Keep in mind, when you are unable to change a situation, you will be challenged to change yourself. If something displeases you, change it. If you are incapable of changing it, change the way you perceive it, until an acceptable alignment can be accomplished. This positive, yet flexible, approach is a key that builds leaders. Those who desire perpetual success must be willing to change with the revolution of the times, for the wheel of change moves on. Good leaders learn to transform their attitudes as they move forward; the great ones influence others to follow along. It has been said, **"Ability is what you're capable of doing. Motivation determines what you do. Attitude determines how well you do it."**

God grant me the serenity to
accept the things I cannot change,
The courage to change the things I can,
and the wisdom to know the difference.
Author Unknown

Gary Bergenske

Campaign To Be A Better Leader

Chapter Eleven

Team Effort Accelerates Success

"When a team outgrows individual performance and learns team confidence, excellence becomes a reality."
Joe Paterno

Cooperatively functioning as a group with a common goal to succeed, under the direction of well-informed leadership, builds winners. Through collaboration, a group will be rewarded for their joint labors. The victories come in a multitude of sizes and value as they build from one to another, until a goal is achieved. More importantly, when you have reached your goal, you will find yourself in a position to see the next hurdle as an extension of the victory. Working as a team brings with it many rewards, including nurturing individual performances for those who work in unison to win championships. Teamwork divides the task and doubles the success.

Brett Farve—I can think of no greater example of a committed team player who himself is a tremendous athlete. Regardless of his talents, he always thinks *"TEAM"* first. He is the preeminent example of an individual who motivates and leads his team. After one season with the Atlanta Falcons, he was traded to the Green Bay Packers. He became the Packer's starting quarterback in the fourth game of the 1992 NFL season. Favre is the *only* three-time Associated Press Most Valuable Player recipient (1995-97) in NFL history, yet remains known for his teamwork.

Farve has led the Packers to two Super Bowls - a victory against the New England Patriots in Super Bowl XXXI and a loss to the Denver Broncos in Super Bowl XXXII. Farve, who played 17 seasons in the NFL, started every game since his first start for the Packers in 1992. His records include: most career NFL touchdown passes; most career NFL interceptions thrown; most consecutive starts among NFL quarterbacks; most career pass completions; most career pass attempts; and most career victories as a starting quarterback.

Brett Farve's passion for his team shines brightly, and his actions speak loudly. Although one of the older players who played in the NFL, he was one of the most enthusiastic in the game. Often, after a pass completion, he would run to congratulate his receivers on their catch. He was a leader within the squad who moved the entire team to become better than even many of them thought they could be. He led by example, one play at a time, one game after another, season by season, team by team, always with the same desired results - to make the team a winner. He was aware that individual talent can at times win a game, but only with teamwork can a championship be won. He is a professional at taking the small wins, and then incorporating them into the big picture. He is a team winner!

In the March 2004 issue of Men's Journal, Farve was chosen as the No.1 'Toughest Guy in America' on the basis of his "fearlessness, perseverance, a willingness to take risk, a tolerance for pain, and even a dash of modesty." These qualities only add to his popularity with teammates and fans. Vince Lombardi, a Green Bay Packer coach decades prior to Farve's time, saw it this way, *"People who work together will win, whether it be against complex football defenses, or the problems of modern society."*

Endurance is one of the most difficult disciplines of teamwork, as you must depend on your teammate's participation. **Victory is achieved by those who endure as a team till the goal is reached.** When a team outgrows individual performance and learns team confidence, excellence becomes reality. An acronym for the word *TEAM* is, **"Together Everyone Accomplishes More."**

Andrew Carnegie said, **"Teamwork is the ability to work together toward a common vision; the ability to direct individual accomplishments toward organizational objectives. It is the fuel that allows common people to attain uncommon results."**

Following are ten key elements needed in developing a team who will work together for the betterment of all concerned:

Ten Keys in Building Teamwork

- **Valued Strategies**
- **Good Communication**
- **Common Positive Goals**
- **Combined Mutual Vision**
- **Defined Leadership Roles**

- **Joint Recovery to Setbacks**
- **Accountability to Each Other**
- **Mutual Respect for Each Other**
- **Support System / Mentally Strong**
- **Avoidance of Conflict / Procrastination**

In building a team using the above guidelines, it soon becomes apparent how much can be accomplished by those who do not care who receives the credit, only that the job has been done successfully. As time moves forward, the team members build on working together, sharing together, and eventually succeeding together, even if working apart at different locations. In the business world, unlike a sports team, the corporate team can extend around the world. They still have the need to work as a team through modern day communications and technologies to be effective, as teamwork cannot be affected by the annoyance of distance.

Great teams come to realize everyone is needed. No one is indispensable. An individual who becomes arrogant, self-centered, or focused on individual talent will become a deterrent to the team. No individual, regardless of his talent, will be an asset to the team if he is not a *"Team Player."* Those who refuse to fit into the team should be removed to enable the team to focus on their goals without any conflicts or negative influences. The strength of the team is in the individual strength of each of the members' combined visions of a successful completion. I can remember as a high school football player our coach telling us to help others to be better, as no one wanted to be considered the weakest link. The path to greatness is found in teamwork, for working together in unity works.

Henry Ford was the founder of the Ford Motor Company. He is the father of the first modern assembly lines where the mass production of large numbers of inexpensive automobiles could be finished in 98 minutes. In his opinion, "**Coming together is a beginning. Keeping together is progress. Working together is success.**" Ford's ability to build teams by way of teamwork within his operation of the car assembly line earned the name "Fordism" in the early 1900's. His knack to build teams allowed him to become one of the richest and best-known individuals in the world.

> **Coming together is a beginning.**
> **Keeping together is progress.**
> **Working together is success.**
> **Henry Ford**

Leaders not only know where they are, but where they are headed. They also know how to persuade other people to follow along. Many individuals are successful in their own world; however, it takes the gifted ones who are competent in performing as a leader of groups or organizations to build a team. Having the wherewithal to build a successful team that works together combined with the personality and professionalism to lead them to great encounters is most rewarding for a leader. Knowing how you influence others builds positive results, fuels them to do more, and can become an inspiration to all members on the team.

A group becomes a team when each member believes in himself enough to readily give praise to others for their contributions. This can begin to snowball as each member rises to the next level due to the motivation received from his counterparts. When people excel on their team, they also feel a strong sense of personal worth. Individual commitment to others is what makes a team.

Gary Bergenske

Recently, I had the honor to attend my nephew, Clayton's, graduation from Marine boot camp at Parris Island, South Carolina. These young men and women, nearly six hundred of them in the class, sent chills up my back as I witnessed them operate in unison as a team. They came from numerous places east of the Mississippi River. For ninety days, they arose at four-thirty in the morning. Knowing no one upon arrival, but with a common goal in mind to succeed and under the direction of some of the finest leadership in the world, they became a team. Being part of the military, they were not allowed to question why; it was their duty to follow the directions of a proven method for success.

They had the requirement to hit the bunks at eight o'clock nightly, with no television, radio, or phone calls; their focus was on making the grade. Living on a structured diet combined with a strenuous physical fitness program caused many of them to lose twenty five to thirty pounds. They would give it all they had within themselves. They focused on becoming one of **"The Few, The Proud."** Each would become a part of this elite team, willing to help each other at all costs and no matter what the circumstances, including war. Every Marine lives by a motto: **"Semper Fidelis"** *("Always Faithful.")* Marines have lived up to this motto, a statement illustrated by the fact that there has never been a mutiny, or even the thought of one, among U.S. Marines.

During their training, recruits pass by a statue inspired by the famous photograph of five Marines and a U.S. Navy corpsman raising the U.S. flag atop the 546 ft Mount Suribachi at the battle of Iwo Jima. The statue represents what was actually the second flag-raising on the mountain, which took place on the fifth day of the 35-day battle. The picture became the iconic image of the battle and may be the most reproduced photograph of all time. Placed at the foot of the statue is a quote from Admiral Nimitz's speech from March 16, 1945, *"Uncommon Valor was a Common Virtue."* It is with this influence these men and women are transformed into Marines, where they will constantly and continually act as a team to protect our nation.

"Uncommon Valor was a Common Virtue"

As I watched the day's events unfold, I could not have been prouder. Not just of my nephew, or of the newly created Marines, but by the entire assemblage. It was a team effort, from the top officer on the base to the recruits who would not graduate with this class, but with a later one. Teamwork, functioning as it only could in this military setting, was operating perfectly. It made me swell with pride to be an American.

Leaders Know their Limits, and the Limits of their Team

Leaders concentrate on finding the superlative portion of different individuals using varied teambuilding activities to best build their team. For example, many portions of a military agenda would not work in a voluntary organization where all of your success depends on the work of volunteers. Those who give of their time cannot be ordered around; they must be influenced and made to feel appreciated. What works in one setting, as good as it may be, can be disastrous in another. As a leader, you must be able to adapt to the current setting.

Great leaders know which leadership skills to use. They know where and how to gain the greatest value. This will give the team the utmost chance to succeed. This type of guidance allows others within the team to grow as leaders, therefore making the team stronger. Team leaders have a responsibility, just like the rest of the team, *to the team first,* regardless of the sacrifices. Teamwork is less me or I, and more we. Leaders remove personal agendas and focus on building the team. In the end, a strong team will reflect back on the leader as an effective and sound performance. A highly seasoned leader or coach will be respected and admired for his willingness to see his team succeed.

Everyone Needs a Team Around Them

Thomas Edison is considered one of the most prolific inventors in history, holding 1,093 U.S. patents in his name, as well as many patents in the United Kingdom, France and Germany. A smart as he was, he needed a team. When asked why he had a team of 21 assistants, he replied, ***"If I could solve all the problems myself, I would."*** Fact is, he needed support from others to accomplish his mission. Having a team allowed for more projects, better ideas, and an enhanced success rate. Teams share the burden and divide the heartache, so they can each have a stake in the gratification. Intelligent people build teams who they become a welcome part of. This accelerates performance, pride, and accomplishments, which in turn encourages learning and behavioral change. Teamwork is the process of give and take for the betterment of the team.

A few years ago my wife, Anne, and I stopped to have lunch on a fall day in North Carolina. The leaves were in full fall color on this October day in the mountains. The small restaurant provided us with good food at a wonderful location. I also found an interesting story titled *"Lessons From Geese"* in the menu by an unknown author. I would like to share this as it relates to **Teamwork**, even by birds.

"Lessons From Geese"

As each goose flaps its wings, it creates an "uplift" for the bird following. By flying in a **V**-formation, the whole flock adds 71% flying range than if each bird flew alone.
Lesson: *People who share a common direction and sense of community can get where they are going quicker and easier because they are traveling on the thrust of one another.*

Whenever a goose falls out of formation it suddenly feels the drag and resistance trying to fly alone, and quickly gets back into formation to take advantage of the "lifting power" of the bird immediately in front.
Lesson: *If we have as much sense as a goose, we will stay in formation with those who are headed where we want to go.*

When the lead goose gets tired, it rotates back into the formation and another goose flies at the point position.
Lesson: *It pays to take turns doing the hard tasks and sharing leadership with people, as with geese, interdependent with each other.*

The geese in formation honk from behind to encourage those up front to keep up their speed.
Lesson: *We need to make sure our honking from behind is encouraging – not something less helpful.*

When a goose gets sick or wounded or shot down, two geese drop out of formation and follow it down to help and protect him. They stay with the goose until it is either able to fly again or dies. Then they launch out on their own with another formation or catch up to the flock.

Gary Bergenske

Lesson: *If we have as much sense as geese, we'll stand by each other like that.*

Author Unknown

Teamwork is found in many companies. In **MonaVie**, a multi-level marketing company that manufactures and distributes a juice made from a blend of fruits, (the most advertised of which is the açaí berry) teamwork is found working around the globe. This company started in 2005, is now the fastest growing company in America reaching sales of $1 billion in its third year of business.

With their team of distributors, **MonaVie** is growing at a phenomenal rate. MonaVie's simple product offering and its rich compensation plan make it one of the most rewarding opportunities in network marketing. They are adding on average an additional 20,000 new distributors to the team weekly. This company is writing a new chapter on teamwork, building a worldwide team marketing a premier product.

In this chapter, I have tried to show the benefits of teamwork are everywhere. Teamwork should be in every aspect of our lives. As illustrated in this chapter, teamwork builds winners in sports, families, the military, volunteer organizations, all size companies, and even between the animals on our planet. Teamwork develops leaders, and then builds winners. Be a team player and enjoy the rewards as a team. Coach Paul *"Bear"* Bryant said, ***"In order to have a winner, the team must have a feeling of unity; every player must put the team first, ahead of personal glory."***

Chapter Twelve

Keeping the Momentum Looking to the Future

"Everyday someone does something great, today that someone will be me."
Lou Holtz

Have you ever wondered why teams or individuals can be World Champions one year and fail miserably the next? Even when returning with the same team and the same coaches, back to back championships are very rare. Teams lose their focus or momentum, or as was said in the 1982 *Rocky III* movie soundtrack, they lose the **"Eye of the Tiger."** It takes special leaders operating consistently to lead others at a high level year after year. Every aspect of leadership must to be maintained in order to carry on at championship status. Few are superior enough or contain the adequate amount of discipline to consistently forge ahead.

The future takes precedence over the past. Past accomplishments are nice, but rarely do they make any substantial distinction in the future without also possessing the correct positive attitude. There is no future in the past. I have seen many teams or businesses fail after great successes simply because they became contentedly complacent. They lost that fire within that inspired the attitude of a winner. John F. Kennedy, the 35th President of the United States, had this to say, **"Change is the law of life. And those who look only to the past or present are certain to miss the future."** The future is where you are headed. The use of your knowledge of the past will determine your wisdom in the future. Couple this with passion and momentum for continued success. Tomorrow belongs to those wise individuals who prepare for it today.

It has been said, "When you look to the future, there are three kinds of people: those who make it happen, those who let it happen, and those who wonder what happened." Individuals who do not dream about the future most likely do not have a plan for where they are going. Leaders must understand what motivates people, how to make them exceed expectations, and what they require to keep the momentum. It's a matter of keeping everything rolling in the right direction once movement has begun. Following are twelve keys to keeping the momentum rolling into the future:

Twelve Keys to Keeping the Momentum Moving

- **Identify Successes**
- **Present New Ideas**
- **Praise Performance**
- **Say Thank You Often**

- **Lean on Your Experts**
- **Believe / Keep the Faith**
- **Know the Team's Abilities**
- **Organize Detailed Reviews**
- **Reflect and Revise Progress**
- **Recognize / Reward Greatness**
- **Acknowledge Accomplishments**
- **Stress Need to Focus on the Future**

When working with these twelve keys, keep the momentum swiftly moving towards the future. I recommend you insist that people are accountable to and willing to share the load. Accountability becomes paramount for continued success. Each person on the team must believe the challenges set forth are realistic. It then becomes essential to set goals for achievement. Each time a significant plateau is reached on the way to the ultimate goal, rewards should be given in celebration of the success. Follow up becomes mandatory to keep everyone on track in order to maintain the momentum for the future. The results must be measurable.

The possibilities of our imagined futures becoming a reality lie in our abilities to pace ourselves to endure the greatest benefits for a successful completion. Moving too quickly can become a deterrent, causing a loss in momentum. Pace yourself! Abraham Lincoln, the sixteenth President of the United States, had this to say about the future, *"The best thing about the future is that it only comes one day at a time."* Along those same lines of not rushing, Albert Einstein, considered the greatest scientist of the twentieth century and one of the supreme intellects of all time, said, *"I never think of the future. It comes soon enough."* Each of us, as leaders, must evaluate and then work at the pace our team works best at to find success in the future.

Gary Bergenske

Your Ability Is Your God Given Talent. Motivation Will Determine How Much You Do. Your Attitude Will Determine How Well You'll Succeed.

Successfully moving into the future while sustaining momentum requires discipline. One thing I believe imperative is for the leader to bring passion and intensity to the team. This is true whether it is a sports team, business organization, family, or any other type of group. Keep in mind - the longer you wait for the future, the shorter it will be, for none of us are getting any younger. Winners learn from the past while they enjoy working in the present, as they travel towards the future. It is best to work on the future, for that is where you will spend the rest of your life.

Looking Into the Future - Kennedy Space Center

Recently, my wife, Anne, and I had an occasion to visit the Kennedy Space Center, America's Spaceport on the East Coast of Florida. There is no other place in the world where history and the future, nature and technology, young and old meet for an inspirational journey through space and time. Due to the fact we were honored guests for the day, we were escorted to areas not normally open to the public. This was an experience we both cherished because of the futuristic mentality of the Spaceport and of those individuals who worked there. This is a place where talk of the Milky Way galaxy, space exploration, the Hubble Space Telescope, Mars, and trips to the moon are just normal conversation. The United States built a space program that has launched men to the Moon, orbited satellites that have improved our lives, and sent probes into distant space to solve the mysteries of the cosmos.

We had the opportunity to walk under the orbiter, ***"Endeavor,"*** that was positioned in a building and was being prepared for its next flight. As we stood under the body of the craft, numerous people were doing inspections and, where needed, replacing the tiles that protect her from the heat of re-entry. Exact precision is vital to the craft and its crew. In a room that was nearly as clean as an operating room, to keep dust at a minimum so not to allow particles to float around when in space, many people worked as a team. With their focus on excellence, in order to provide the safest vehicle possible for our astronauts, their passion to obtain perfection was obvious.

As we moved through two more security check points, we arrived at NASA's launch pad 39A. We drove up to the space shuttle, **"*Atlantis,*"** that was in position on the launch pad for its twenty-fourth mission to the International Space Station. Liftoff was scheduled for four days later. The mere thought of standing next to this vehicle which had many times carried men and women into the depths of space was an inspiration of what the future holds for us. To think of the many accomplishments needed to get the space program to where it is today is mind boggling, seemingly almost impossible. However, by taking the required steps, what seemed impossible a few short years ago has been attained, and now it is the norm.

It was as though everything I have written about in this book was contained in this futuristic place, the Kennedy Space Center. Leadership was paramount, their vision and missions were established, and their passion, persistence, and loyalty were so superior, they stood unquestioned. In this place, the smallest error could mean the death of those traveling into space, so excellence and teamwork were mandatory beyond a shadow of a doubt. Perfection is strived for as they continually look to the future.

Gary Bergenske

The Past Contributes to the Activities of Today, As Great Changes are Developed for fhe Future to Accomplish the Missions of Tomorrow. The Momentum Must Keep Moving!

Even with the cutting edge, ultra-modern tempo, the space program is *changing*. Innovation is needed at all levels, even the most advanced, if they are to continue to grow. The entire space team knows the shuttle program will be phased out in a couple of years, to be replaced by a new type of space vehicle. **Change** - it is needed at every plateau if improvement and growth are to be found. Never in my life have I been somewhere where the past has contributed so much to the activities of today, and where the changes for the future are so great in order to accomplish the missions of tomorrow. The American Space Program exemplifies what can be accomplished when leadership, passion, and teamwork are aligned—excellence.

I came away with the following lesson. No matter what level the playing field, *leaders look for changes to improve the future* while keeping energy and development moving forward. Every American should be proud of the United States Space Program. It exemplifies every characteristic of properly looking into the future to discover the unknown and to do the seemingly impossible. NASA turns science fiction ideas into science fact as they travel through space in search of extraterrestrial life. I can think of no greater example of a place where technology, combined with desire, can lead to more discoveries than the space program. It is phenomenal!

Leaders Prepare for the Future with a Succession Plan

Great leaders look beyond today, regardless of how good things seem. An organization or team can be invincible today, but the loss of a key player or employee tomorrow can cause the organization to look differently. Leaders who have the organization's future success at heart plan for the replacement of people. This can happen in the event of members leaving or even dying. The greatest of leaders go so far as to plan for their own replacement, knowing they, as well, cannot survive forever. It takes a strong, confident leader to mentor and to train his own replacement. This is what separates the good from the great; their commitment to plan for every possible future contingency, including their own demise.

Leaders are willing to make the sacrifices today to develop tomorrow. They understand there is a price to pay for lasting success in any organization. There must be a planned succession arrangement system that is ready to activate quickly when needed. Whether it is a small family business, a college football team, a Fortune 500 company, or the Presidential office of the United States, a plan of succession is required. Good planning provides a seamless transition. This takes away the rough edges and smoothes out the evolution of the team. Conversions of this type bring continuity in the organization, which brings success in the future.

Having worked for years in an environment of volunteer organizations where the top leader changes yearly, I can really identify with this. The leaders who are in it for ***themselves*** seldom work with those around them to help in mentoring others for the future. They quit doing the programs that worked in the past because it is now all about them. These leaders will lose momentum, loyalty, and support; soon, their influence during their year in office will begin to deteriorate. Their followers will begin to feel uninspired as the organization begins to have difficulty looking to the future. The momentum is lost, and so is the excitement.

On the contrary, those leaders who are in it for the ***organization*** build hope for the future. They continue successful, old traditions, try new ideas and events, and build team morale. These leaders assist others in achieving their dreams. They ignite the desire of people to move forward in the organization, giving them the inspiration to be part of the future. This brings added value to being a member by allowing them to feel important and needed. They will take ownership in the organization. Individuals will begin to plan for and benchmark future goals with the blessing of the leader. ***Leaders who care are not threatened by others moving forward;*** they promote it for the betterment of the organization.

Leaders Assist Others in Achieving Their Dreams

A truly great leader desires those who follow him to do even better. He also feels a small, humble part because he has helped them, all for the future of the organization. Leaders are judged by the group's achievements and those they have inspired, not by what they have achieved individually. The leaders who have played the game correctly and with the best interest for the future of the organization in mind will leave office with respect, integrity, and many friends. This may be the truest test of the success of leaders. In a volunteer setting, where everyone works to get encouragement, to receive thanks, and to earn heart-felt rewards, true leaders shine.

Many years ago, I ran across a poem that has inspired me to keep on moving forward, regardless of how tough things may seem. For the past thirty years, I have, from time to time, hung it next to my desk. I'd like to share it with you. Never let your momentum stop.

Don't Quit

When things go wrong, as they sometimes will,
When the road you're trudging seems all uphill,
When the funds are low and the debts are high,
And you want to smile, but you have to sigh,
    When care is pressing you down a bit . . .
    Rest if you must, but don't you quit.

Life is queer with its twists and turns,
As every one of us sometimes learns,
And many a fellow turns about
When he might have won had he stuck it out.
Don't give up though the pace seems slow . . .
    You may succeed with another blow.

Often the goal is nearer than
It seems to a faint and faltering man;
Often the struggler has given up
When he might have captured the victor's cup;
And he learned too late when the night came down
How close he was to the golden crown.

Success is failure turned inside out ---
The silver tint of the clouds of doubt,
And you never can tell how close you are,
It may be near when it seems afar;
So stick to the fight when you're hardest hit,
It's when things seem worst that you mustn't quit.

Author Unknown

Gary Bergenske

Conclusion

The twelve keys to leadership discussed in this book will develop you into a successful leader, but only if you practice and live by them. Great leaders are always looking for other ways to make themselves and those around them better. They are committed to life-long learning. Leaders dream big and realize opportunity is everywhere, if they take the time to find and develop it. Keep in mind—*attitude* is the key factor that will drive your success. Keep your attitude positive, and everything else will become easier.

I wrote **Campaign to be a Better Leader** with the hope it would help many people become more inspired to step up their leadership abilities. I firmly believe every leader has within them the ability to change the direction of their organization for the better, if only he or she strives for excellence. When you look at the bottom line, empowering leadership is what gives one organization the advantage over another.

Keep chasing your dreams. Become the leader you were meant to be. Your influence on others will become your greatest legacy as it builds better lives.

I would ask you to practice the following ten steps as you work at becoming a better leader:

Ten Steps to Becoming a Better Leader

1. Make the commitment to follow through on developing these essential tools in making yourself a better leader.

2. Believe in everything you do, in yourself, in your organization, and in your followers.

3. Become a person who strives to attain excellence. Help others do the same by influencing them.

4. Be open-minded and have vision that is guided towards success. Live by the Golden Rule.

5. Give yourself to others by mentoring them to be their best. Be complimentary.

6. Communicate thoroughly and enthusiastically, so others will be well informed and inspired.

7. Allow your passions to grow with never-ending contagiousness. Be a leader others want to be associated with.

8. Never back-slide. Be persistent. Persevere until your mission is accomplished, regardless of what others say.

9. Look for change. Remember, future successes, as of yet undreamed of, will develop from the effects of what we do today.

10. Build a team to lead. Nothing great has ever been done without the help of others.

Leaders are the champions of their game. They may rise and fall with the challenges they face, but they have the wherewithal to continue the chase for success. True leaders are the professionals in their field who know how to inspire others to attain their personal best, time and time again.

Leaders become great because they work at it. They may have talent, but without great will-power to push their talent, mediocrity sets in. Leaders develop confidence and persevere to obtain what they believe in at any cost. Life is built on experiences that make us who we are. The choices we make determine the type of person we are and will become. These things also determine the type of leader we will grow to be. Do what it takes. Turn into the type of leader you've dreamed to be.

Now that you have completed this book, I wish you the best. **You can and will become a better leader if you truly desire to do so.** Read, learn, and practice; continue to influence others in a positive way and good fortune will be your friend. May God bless you and your efforts in becoming a ***Better Leader***, and in building better leaders for our future.

> *"Destiny is not a matter of chance;*
> *it is a matter of choice.*
> *It is not something to be waited for;*
> *but rather something to be achieved."*
> **William Jennings Bryan**

Gary Bergenske

About the Author

Gary Bergenske was born in Madison, Wisconsin, in 1954 and was raised in Pardeeville, a small nearby town. After graduating from Portage High School, his family moved to Jacksonville, Florida. Never having attended college, Gary began his career working in restaurants and selling insurance for Northwestern Mutual, becoming one of their youngest million dollar sellers at the age of 21.

In 1985, he pursued his dream of owning his own business by purchasing J & J Metro Moving and Storage Co. in Orlando, Florida. As the company's President/Owner, three years later he purchased a competitor's business. He has continued to grow his company the past 23 years by purchasing an additional three competitors in Florida, by building relationships with key accounts, and by providing nationwide service. Gary leads others in the same way he lives and manages his own life - with desire and passion. His success has been self-made, and his mission is to influence others in a positive way.

A motivational speaker, he has delivered his inspirational message at engagements through out the United States on leadership, teamwork, and mentoring. In 2005, he served as Potentate of Bahia Shriners in Orlando, Florida. He is currently serving as a member of the Boards of Directors for Shriners of North America and Shriners Hospitals for Children. Bergenske was elected during the Shriners' 2007 annual international convention – or Imperial Council Session – held in Anaheim, Calif. He is serving as part of the 13-member body that helps govern the Shriners' fraternity.

His focus is in helping others reach their full leadership potential. His inspiring book, **Campaign For A Better Life,** was released in March of 2007 and is a great example of how he wishes to help the lives of others grow in character with integrity.

Gary and Anne, his wife, have six children aged 20 to 30. The children, three boys and three girls, are often referred to as the Bergy Bunch. The family maintains a vacation home on Daytona Beach. Gary loves and collects antique automobiles, but his favorite recreation vehicle is a Harley Davidson.

Campaign To Be A Better Leader

Contact the Author

You can contact Gary Bergenske at:

**Gary Bergenske
1101 West Kennedy Boulevard
Orlando, Florida 32810**

**Phone: 407-875-0000
FAX: 407-875-0480**

GBergenske@aol.com

Visit Gary Bergenske's Website at:

www.Garymotivations.com
or
www.ShrinerGary.com

To arrange a speaking engagement for Gary Bergenske, please write him at the above address, or call **407-875-0000**. Requests can also be faxed to **407-875-0480**, or e-mailed to Gary Bergenske at **GBergenske@aol.com.**

We would enjoy hearing from you. Please send your comments on this book to Gary Bergenske at the above address.

We appreciate you and hope you begin ***Campaign "ing" to be a Better Leader*** immediately!

To purchase additional copies of ***Campaign to be a Better Leader*** or its sister book ***Campaign For A Better Life,*** also by Gary Bergenske, contact your favorite bookstore or go online to **www.GaryMotivations.com.** You may also fax your order to **(407) 875-0480**. Discounts are available for multiple book purchases by contacting Gary Bergenske.

Campaign To Be A Better Leader

Be sure to order Gary's first book in this series:

Campaign for a Better Life

Available in:
Hard cover
Paperback:
Audio CD]

Order online at: www.GaryMotivations.com
or you may fax your order to: (407) 875-0480

Discounts are available for multiple book purchases by contacting Gary Bergenske at: 407-875-0000

www.ingramcontent.com/pod-product-compliance
Lightning Source LLC
Chambersburg PA
CBHW022134080426
42734CB00006B/356